Before the altar a r

He is dressed in the costume of a ninja, but red in colour and without the hood. A black cloth belt is tied around his waist. His forearms are exposed. A scorpion is tattooed on each wrist. His face is nondescript, instantly forgettable, save for the eyes, black as night and full of power and malice. On the floor in front of him rests an unusual weapon, a kyoketsu-shoze. A length of braided animal hair connects a heavy metal ring to a dagger-like blade.

'Welcome, Avenger,' he says, his voice blank and unaccented, so that it could not be recognised again. 'I did not expect you to get this far. You have done well. But now you have come to the end. I am the Grandmaster of Shadows, Master of the Way of the Scorpion, the supreme form of ninjutsu. No mere adept am I, but the most accomplished ninja on Orb.'

Gamebooks from Fabled Lands Publishing

by Jamie Thomson and Dave Morris:

Fabled Lands 1: The War-Torn Kingdom
Fabled Lands 2: Cities of Gold and Glory
Fabled Lands 3: Over the Blood-Dark Sea
Fabled Lands 4: The Plains of Howling Darkness
Fabled Lands 5: The Court of Hidden Faces
Fabled Lands 6: Lords of the Rising Sun

by Dave Morris:

Heart of Ice
Down Among the Dead Men
Necklace of Skulls
Once Upon a Time in Arabia
Crypt of the Vampire
The Temple of Flame
The Castle of Lost Souls

by Oliver Johnson:

Curse of the Pharaoh
The Lord of Shadow Keep

by Dave Morris and Oliver Johnson:

Blood Sword 1: The Battlepits of Krarth

by Jamie Thomson and Mark Smith:

Way of the Tiger 1: Avenger
Way of the Tiger 2: Assassin
Way of the Tiger 3: Usurper
Way of the Tiger 4: Overlord

In preparation:

Way of the Tiger 5: Warbringer
Way of the Tiger 6: Inferno
Blood Sword 2: The Kingdom of Wyrd

Way of the Tiger
OVERLORD!

JAMIE THOMSON
& MARK SMITH

FL

Originally published 1986 by Knight Books
This edition published 2014 by Fabled Lands Publishing
an imprint of Fabled Lands LLP

www.sparkfurnace.com

Illustrations by Hokusai, Aude Pfister, Mylène Villeneuve,
Dominique Gilis, Maria Nikolopoulou and Antoine Di Lorenzo

Edited by Richard S. Hetley

With thanks to Mikaël Louys, Michael Spencelayh, Paul Gresty
and David Walters

ISBN-13: 978-1-909905-13-9
ISBN-10: 1909905135

WARNING!

Do not attempt any of the techniques or methods described in this book. They could result in serious injury or death to an untrained user.

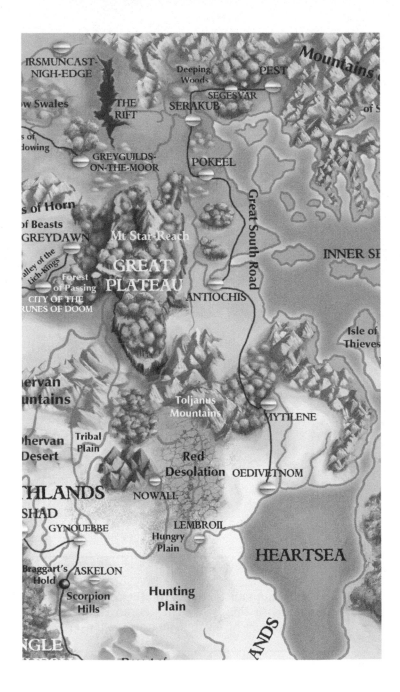

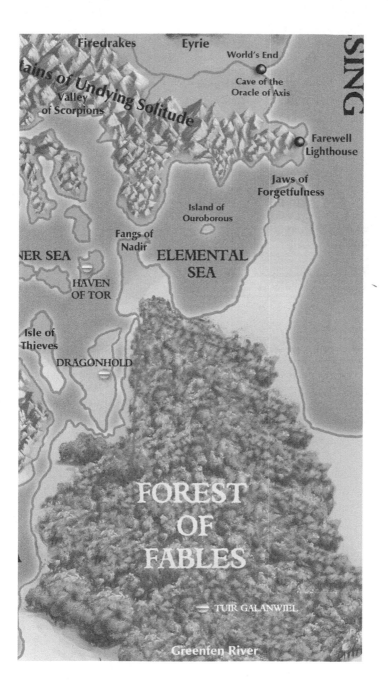

Adventure Gamebooks

Ninja Character Sheet

Combat Ratings								
Punch	O							
Kick	O							
Throw	O							
Fate Modifier	O							

Skills   + Shurikenjutsu

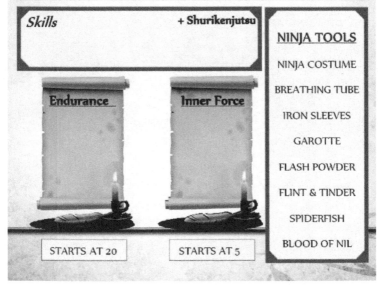

Endurance

Inner Force

STARTS AT 20

STARTS AT 5

NINJA TOOLS

NINJA COSTUME

BREATHING TUBE

IRON SLEEVES

GAROTTE

FLASH POWDER

FLINT & TINDER

SPIDERFISH

BLOOD OF NIL

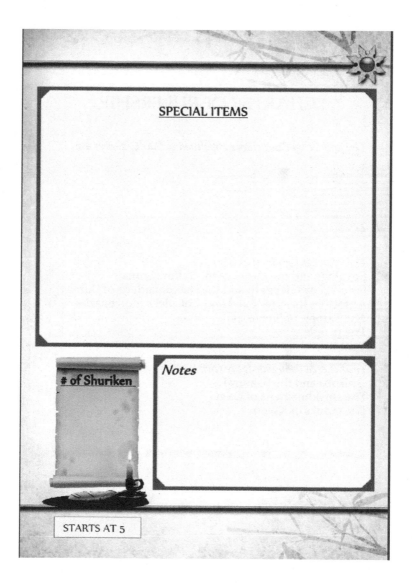

SPECIAL ITEMS

of Shuriken

Notes

STARTS AT 5

CHARTER OF RULERSHIP

The four Privy Councillors appointed to Star Chamber are:

1.

2.

3.

4.

The Watch is kept by (tick one):
Foxglove and the Order of the Yellow Lotus ☐
Force-Lady Gwyneth and the shieldmaidens of Dama ☐
Antocidas the One-Eyed and Golspiel's mercenaries ☐
The Temple of Nemesis ☐
The people ☐

Your chosen bodyguards are (tick one):
Onikaba and the Samurai ☐
The shieldmaidens of Dama ☐
The monks of Kwon ☐

The army is composed of (tick one or two):
The Usurper's army ☐
Force-Lady Gwyneth and the shieldmaidens of Dama ☐
Citizen militia led by the Demagogue ☐

Taxes and funds in the
treasury equal _____ talents
   minus Crown costs _____ talents
   equals effect on popularity _____ (subtract this figure from your Popularity Rating)

Popularity Rating   **Starts at 2**

Winged Horse Kick

Leaping Tiger Kick

1

2

Forked Lightning Kick

Iron Fist Punch

Tiger's Paw Punch

Cobra Strike
Punch

Whirlpool Throw

Dragon's Tail Throw

Teeth of Tiger Throw

THE WAY OF THE TIGER

Adventure Gamebooks

Opponent Encounter Boxes

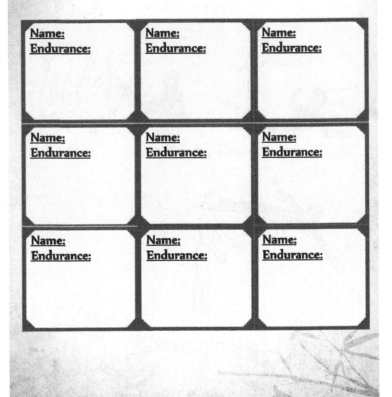

Name:
Endurance:

Name:
Endurance:

Name:
Endurance:

Name:
Endurance:

Name:
Endurance:

Name:
Endurance:

Name:
Endurance:

Name:
Endurance:

Name:
Endurance:

BACKGROUND

On the magical world of Orb, alone in a sea that the people of the Manmarch call Endless, lies the mystical Island of Tranquil Dreams.

Many years have passed since the time when you first saw its golden shores and emerald rice meadows. A servant brought you, braving the distant leagues of the ponderous ocean from lands to which you have never returned. Your loyal servant laid you, an orphan, at the steps of the Temple of the Rock praying that the monks would care for you, for she was frail and dying of a hideous curse.

Monks have lived on the island for centuries, dedicated to the worship of their God, Kwon, He who speaks the Holy Words of Power, Supreme Master of Unarmed Combat. They live only to help others resist the evil that infests the world. Seeing that you were alone and needed care, the monks took you in and you became an acolyte at the Temple of the Rock. Nothing was made of the strange birthmark, shaped like a crown, which you carry on your thigh, though you remember that the old servant insisted that it was of mystical importance. Whenever you have asked about this the monks have bade you meditate and be patient.

The most ancient and powerful of them all, Naijishi, Grandmaster of the Dawn, became your foster-father. He gave you guidance and training in the calm goodness of Kwon, knowledge of men and their ways and how to meditate so that your mind floats free of your body and rides the winds in search of truth.

From the age of six, however, most of your time has been spent learning the Way of the Tiger. Now you are a ninja, a master of the martial arts and a deadly assassin who can kill the most powerful enemies unseen and unsuspected. Like a tiger, you are strong, stealthy, agile, patient in the stalking of prey and deadly. On the Island of Plenty and in the Manmarch the fabled ninja, known as the 'Men with no Shadow', are held in awe – the mere mention of ninja strikes fear into people's hearts. But you are one of the few who worship Kwon and follow the Way of the Tiger. You use your skill as a bringer of death to rid the world of evil-doers.

At an early age you hung by the hands for hours on end from the branches of trees to strengthen your arms. You ran for miles, your light-footed speed enough to keep a thirty-foot ribbon trailing above the ground. You trod tightropes, as agile as a monkey. Now you swim like a fish and leap like a tiger, you move like the whisper of the breeze and glide through the blackest night like a shade. Before he died, Naijishi taught you the Ninja's Covenant.

NINJA NO CHIGIRI

'I will vanish into the night; change my body to wood or stone; sink into the earth and walk through walls and locked doors. I will be killed many times, yet will not die; change my face and become invisible, able to walk among men without being seen.'

It was after your foster-father Naijishi's death that you began to live the words of the Covenant. A man came to the island: Yaemon, Grandmaster of Flame. Using borrowed sorcery he tricked the monks into believing that he was a worshipper of Kwon from the Greater Continent. He was indeed a monk but he worshipped Kwon's twisted brother, Vile, who helps the powerful to subdue the weak and wicked men to rule fools. Yaemon slew Naijishi – no one could match him in unarmed combat – and he stole the Scrolls of Kettsuin from the Temple. Once more you knew the pain of loss for you had loved Naijishi as a father. You swore an oath to Kwon that one day you would avenge his death... and you *were* avenged. Now after many adventures you are set to further unravel the skein of your destiny.

THE NEW OVERLORD

The first-born of your family for four generations have carried the mark of the missionary king, and your birth father was Overlord of a great city in the Manmarch, Irsmuncast nigh Edge. Now it is night but the tumult of celebration in the city continues unabated, for today you have regained your rightful crown. The Usurper of Irsmuncast, a foul demon who was turning the city to evil, has been cast down by your own hand and now you must rule in his place.

Weary but exultant, you climb to the topmost turret of the Palace to survey the city. Palace Road, a wide avenue of lime trees, leads past the houses of the well-to-do to a grand crossroads with Cross Street. East of here two buildings dwarf all others save the Palace itself. The brooding black pinnacles of the temple to Nemesis, the Supreme Principle of Evil, Lord of the Cleansing Flame, seem to claw rapaciously at the glowing sky. One of the many difficulties of your rule will be to keep the templars of Nemesis in check.

Equally imposing is the great, grey fortress pyramid that is the Temple to Dama, Shieldmaiden of the Gods. The warrior women who serve it were valiant law keepers under the rule of your father, Loremaster Szeged. Smaller than these and opposite the black pinnacles is the white stone Temple to Avatar, Supreme Principle of Good. A great white torch flares atop the spire's cross in your honour.

In the distance to the south-east is the area of blackness which denotes the park where lies the temple to your own god, Kwon the Redeemer. Nearby are the many coloured lights of the merchants' quarter. The people in the streets who rose up under the urging of the Demagogue, their leader, to throw off the Usurper's yoke are still chanting your name as you turn to the west and north, where all is strangely quiet. The huge Temple to Time stands dark against the stillness and the inscrutable priests of that most powerful of gods show no sign either of welcome or rejection. How much time will be vouchsafed you to rule over Irsmuncast nigh Edge, the last bastion of men before the Rift? Irsmuncast holds back the black tide which threatens to swamp the lands of men.

The east side of the city is named the Edgeside. The city wall here is taller than at any other point because it faces the Rift – the Bowels of Orb – from which nameless evil issues forth to pollute Orb. You must play your part in keeping this evil in check. Your exultation fades as weariness overcomes you. In the morning you must be Overlord. For now you must sleep.

RULES OF COMBAT

As a master of Taijutsu, the ninja's art of unarmed combat, you have four main ways of fighting: throwing shuriken (see under skills), kicks, punches and throws.

In general it will be harder to hit an opponent when kicking but a kick will do more damage than a punch. A throw, if successful, will allow you to follow up with a possible 'killing blow', but if you fail a throw your Defence against an opponent will be lower, as you are open to attack. Shuriken are a special case and will be mentioned in the text when you can use them.

Whenever you are in a combat you will be asked which type of attack you wish to make. See the Way of the Tiger illustrations for the different types of kicks, punches and throws available to you. Think about your opponent and its likely fighting style. Trying to throw a giant enemy is not going to be as easy as throwing an ordinary man, for example. You will be told which paragraph to turn to, depending on your choice.

When you are resolving combat, you will find it useful to record your opponent's current Endurance score. A number of Encounter Boxes are provided with your Character Sheet for this purpose.

The combats have been presented in such a way that it is possible for you to briefly examine the rules and begin play almost immediately, but fighting is tactical. Do not forget the rules for blocking and Inner Force (see below), as you will rarely be told when to use these in the text.

PUNCH

When you try to strike an enemy with a punch, that enemy will have a Defence number. You need to score higher than this number on the roll of two dice (an Attack Roll). You get to add your Punch Modifier (see below) to this roll. If the score is higher than his or her Defence number, you have punched your opponent successfully. In this case, roll one more die. The result is the amount of damage you have inflicted on your opponent. Every opponent has Endurance or 'hit points'. The damage you do is subtracted from your opponent's Endurance total. If this has reduced your opponent's score to 0 or less, you have won.

Punch Modifier: Whenever you make an Attack Roll to determine whether or not you have successfully punched an opponent, add or subtract your Punch Modifier. This number reflects your skill in using the punches of the Way of the Tiger. Your starting Punch Modifier is 0, as noted on your Character Sheet. This may change during the adventure.

The Enemy's Attack: After you punch, any opponent still in the fight will counter attack. You will be given your Defence number. Roll two dice, and if the score is greater than your Defence, you have been hit. The amount of damage inflicted upon you depends on the opponent and will be noted in the text, in a format such as 'Damage: 1 Die + 1' or '2 Dice' or '1 Die + 2'. Simply roll the required number of dice and add any other number given. This is the total damage inflicted upon you. However, before you subtract this score from your Endurance, you may choose to try and block or parry the attack (see block) to prevent any damage.

KICK
The kick and the Kick Modifier work exactly as the punch, except that a kick will do 2 more points of damage than a punch ('1 Die + 2'). It will often be harder to hit with a kick. If the opponent survives, he or she will counter attack.

THROW
The throw and Throw Modifier work as the punch to determine success. A throw does no damage to your foe; instead, you will be allowed another attack, a punch or kick, with a +2 bonus to hit (like an extra Punch Modifier or Kick Modifier) and +2 to damage. (All bonuses are cumulative – a kick normally does '1 Die + 2' damage, so after a successful throw it does '1 Die + 4'.) The opponent will only counter attack against a throw if you fail.

ENDURANCE

You begin the game with 20 points of Endurance. Keep a running total of your Endurance on your Character Sheet. It will probably be the number that will change most as you are wounded, healed etc. When you reach 0 Endurance or less, you are dead and your adventure ends. When restoring Endurance, you cannot go above your maximum of 20.

BLOCK

As a ninja, a master of Taijutsu, you have the ability to block or parry incoming blows with various parts of your body, often your forearms. For this purpose, thin lightweight iron rods have been sewn into your sleeves enabling you to block even swords and other weapons. During combat, if you have been hit, you may try to block the blow and take no damage. Roll two dice. If the score is less than your Defence given in that combat, you have successfully blocked the blow, and take no damage. If your score is equal to or greater than your Defence, you take damage in the normal way. In any case, because you have taken the time to block, your next attack will be less effective, as your opponent has had more time to react. Whether your block is successful or not, −2 will be applied to your Punch, Kick and Throw Modifier for your next attack only. Remember, you can only block blows, not missiles or magic.

INNER FORCE

You begin the game with 5 points of Inner Force. Through meditation and rigorous training you have mastered the ability to unleash spiritual or inner power through your body in the same way as the karate experts of today break blocks of wood and bricks. In any combat, before you roll the dice to determine if you will hit or miss an opponent, you may choose to use Inner Force. If you do, deduct one point from your Inner Force score. This is used up whether or not you succeed in striking your opponent. If you are successful, however, double the damage you inflict – first make your roll for damage and add any bonus (e.g., '1 Die + 2' for a kick), then double the result. When your Inner Force is reduced to

0, you cannot use Inner Force again until you find some way to restore it – so use it wisely. When restoring Inner Force, you cannot go above your maximum of 5.

FATE

Luck plays its part and the goddess Fate has great power on the world of Orb. Whenever you are asked to make a Fate Roll, roll two dice, adding or subtracting your Fate Modifier. If the score is 7–12, you are lucky and Fate has smiled on you. If the score is 2–6, you are unlucky and Fate has turned her back on you. You begin your adventure with a Fate Modifier of 0. Later on, this might go up or down, as you are blessed or cursed by Fate.

NINJA TOOLS

As well as any equipment you may take depending on your skills (see next), as a ninja you have certain tools with you from the beginning. These are:

THE NINJA COSTUME

During the day you would normally be disguised as a traveller, beggar or suchlike. At night when on a mission, you would wear costume. This consists of a few pieces of black cloth. One piece is worn as a jacket covering the chest and arms, two others are wound around each leg and held in at the waist. Finally, a long piece of cloth is wrapped around the head, leaving only the eyes exposed. The reverse side of the costume can be white, for travel on snowy ground, or green, for travel in woods or grasslands.

IRON SLEEVES

Sewn into the sleeves of your costume are four thin strips of iron, the length of your forearm. These allow you to parry or block blows from swords and other cutting weapons.

BREATHING TUBE

Made from bamboo, this can be used as a snorkel allowing you to remain underwater for long periods of time. It can also be used as a blow-pipe in conjunction with the Poison Needles skill, for added range.

GARROTTE

A specialised killing tool of the ninja, this is a length of wire used to assassinate enemies by strangulation.

FLASH POWDER

This powder, when thrown in any source of flame, causes a blinding flash. You have enough for one use only.

FLINT AND TINDER

Used for making fires.

SPIDERFISH

Salted and cured, this highly venomous fish is used as a source for the deadly poison used in conjunction with the Poison Needles skill, and as a useful way of removing any guardian beasts or animals.

THE BLOOD OF NIL

You also carry one dose of the most virulent poison known on Orb. This venom is extremely difficult and very dangerous to collect for it is taken from the barb of a scorpion son of the God, Nil, Mouth of the Void. You had used yours long ago, but have found a replacement amongst the bizarre and otherworldly treasures hoarded by the evil Usurper.

THE SKILLS OF THE WAY OF THE TIGER

You have been trained in ninjutsu almost all of your life. Your senses of smell, sight and hearing have been honed to almost superhuman effectiveness. You are well versed in woodcraft, able to track like a bloodhound, and to cover your own tracks. Your knowledge of plants and herb lore enables you to live off the land. You are at the peak of physical fitness, able to run up to 50 miles a day and swim like a fish. Your training included horsemanship, a little ventriloquism, meditation, the ability to hold yourself absolutely still for hours on end, perfecting your balance, and 'The Seven Ways of Going' or disguise. The latter skill involves comprehensive training so that you can perform as a minstrel, for instance, if this disguise is used. However, a major part of this training has been stealth, hiding in shadows, moving silently, and breathing as quietly as possible, enabling you to move about unseen and unheard. You begin the game with these skills.

There are nine other skills. One of these, Shurikenjutsu, is always taught to a ninja in training. This you must take, but you may then choose three other skills from the remaining eight, and note them on your Character Sheet.

SHURIKENJUTSU

You begin the adventure with five shuriken. The type you specialise in are 'throwing stars', small razor-sharp star-shaped disks of metal. You can throw these up to a range of about thirty feet with devastating effect. If you throw a shuriken, you will be given a Defence number for your target. Roll two dice, and if the score is higher than the Defence number, you will have hit your target. The text will describe the damage done. You may find yourself in a position where you are unable to retrieve a shuriken once you have thrown it. Keep a running total in the box provided on your Character Sheet, crossing off a shuriken each time you lose one. If you have none left, you can no longer use this skill. You are free to carry as many as you find in your adventures.

ARROW CUTTING

Requiring excellent muscular co-ordination, hand and eye judgment and reflexes, this skill will enable you to knock aside, or even catch, missiles such as arrows or spears.

ACROBATICS

The ability to leap and jump using flips, cartwheels, etc, like a tumbler or gymnast.

IMMUNITY TO POISONS

This involves taking small doses of virulent poisons over long periods of time, slowly building up the body's resistance. This enables you to survive most poison attempts.

FEIGNING DEATH

Requiring long and arduous training, a ninja with this ability is able to slow down heart rate and metabolism through will power alone, thus appearing to be dead.

ESCAPOLOGY

A ninja with this skill is able to dislocate the joints of the body and to maximise the body's suppleness, allowing movement through small spaces, and escape from bonds and chains by slipping out of them.

POISON NEEDLES

Sometime known as Spitting Needles, with this skill you can place small darts, coated with a powerful poison that acts in the blood stream, onto your tongue. By curling the tongue into an 'O' shape and spitting or blowing, the dart can be propelled up to an effective range of about 15 feet. A useful surprise attack, the source of which is not always perceptible.

PICKING LOCKS, DETECTING AND DISARMING TRAPS

The ability to open locked doors, chests etc. With this skill you would carry various lockpicks in the pockets of your costume, including a small crowbar or jemmy. You are also trained to notice traps and to use the lock-picking tools to disarm them.

CLIMBING

Comprehensive training in the use of a grappling hook and hand and foot clamps, or cat's claws. The padded four-pronged hook has forty feet of rope attached to it. Used to hook over walls, niches etc, allowing you to pull yourself up the rope. The cat's claws are spiked clamps, worn over the palm of the hands and the instep of the feet, enabling you to embed your claws into a wall and climb straight up like a fly, and even to crawl across ceilings.

SPECIAL RULES FOR THIS BOOK

The Charter of Rulership will help you to play through this adventure as the ruler of the City of Irsmuncast. Use it to keep track of the decisions which you make. The part of the Charter dealing with taxes and popularity will be explained as you read through the book.

If you have not played and successfully completed Book 3: *USURPER!* in the Way of the Tiger series then you begin this book with the equipment and skills listed. If you have successfully completed Book 3 then you should continue with the same character. Simply transfer all the information on your original Character Sheet to the one given here. You will carry five shuriken again, your flash powder will be replaced if you used it, and your Endurance and Inner Force will have been restored after some rest and the ministering of the court surgeon. Upon inspecting the personal effects of the late Usurper, you find a replacement for your Blood of Nil. You also continue Book 4 with any special items you may have picked up in your journey to the City of Irsmuncast nigh Edge, and do not forget to transfer all your Punch, Kick, etc, Modifiers to your new Character Sheet. You may also have learnt just one of the following two superior skills, taught by the Grandmaster of the Dawn at the Temple of the Rock:

SHINREN

Also called the Training of the Heart, ShinRen is a secret knowledge passed on during several weeks in the hills of the

Island of Tranquil Dreams. You have learned iron control of your emotions; you can walk over glowing coals without turning a hair, endure heat, cold, wind, rain, hunger, thirst and pain that would send a normal person mad. Your instincts have been honed so that you may 'read' any person like an open book – having learnt the language that the body talks, understanding what people think by observing their mannerisms and the way they breathe, the roving of their eyes and their stance. You are able to understand a complicated situation at a glance and act, seizing any opening and taking any chance that appears.

YUBI-JUTSU

Also known as Nerve-Striking. You have learnt how to maim and kill with even quite light blows to vital nerve centres – a technique especially useful when beset by many adversaries at once, or against a formidable human foe. You know the anatomy of man in fine detail, the unprotected points and nerve centres where an accurate blow can stun or even kill.

When you are ready to begin the adventure, turn to **1**.

The magnificent royal bedroom is not decorated to suit your tastes. Although the bed is decked with sable furs and satin sheets, the walls are hung with paintings of souls in torment. Ordering the beautiful handmaiden who brings you balm to turn these to the wall, you sink gratefully into the furs. The High Grandmaster of the Temple to Kwon himself will sleep in the antechamber and his monks will stand guard outside your door. Drifting into slumber you think back to the crowning ceremony. Keeping your composure had taxed you sorely after the terrible struggle with the Usurper and his minions, summoned from the depths of the Abyss. The coming of the mightiest people of the city to do obeisance before you seems little more than a dream, but tomorrow you begin the trials of your reign in earnest.

The first day of the month of Harvest Bounty dawns fine. You awake refreshed and the dark and graceful Palace handmaidens, evidently chosen by the Usurper or his Lord High Steward for their beauty, assist you to bathe and dress. They wait on you hand and foot but you cannot tell if their murmured admiration of your toned body is genuine or mere sycophantic toadying. You breakfast alone with Parsifal, the High Grandmaster of the Temple to Kwon, who explains that the customs ordained by your father, the Loremaster, for his successor dictate the order of happenings on this, your first full day as Overlord of Irsmuncast. The Loremaster did not, of course, rule unaided; he depended on four advisers who sat with him in the Privy Council of Star Chamber. Parsifal ends, 'All those who wish to be considered for the posts of Privy Councillors of Star Chamber must present themselves before you in your Throne Room this very morning.'

As you process solemnly towards the Throne Room, followed by the monks of Kwon and those few of the Usurper's courtiers who have not fled, Parsifal explains the procedure: 'All those who wish to be considered for the honour of being your personal advisers are waiting in the vestibule. Tradition demands that they be presented to you in the order in which they arrived. They will enter the

Throne Room one by one and you, Your Majesty, shall decide whether they take a seat in Star Chamber or leave the Palace in disappointment. Remember, only four may become Privy Councillors.'

Turn to **41**.

2

As fast as you are able, you ascend the wall of the valley to the west until you are high in the mountains once more. After a long and arduous climb through the cold inhospitable Mountains of Undying Solitude, you begin the descent on the other side. Eventually, you have arrived at the foothills. You travel on, trotting constantly for miles across the barren wilderness, until you come to more fertile lands. A faint smell of the sea comes to your nostrils and you head towards it, knowing you must find transport across the Inner Sea. The journey takes several days and passes uneventfully. You may restore up to 5 points of lost Endurance for your restful nights.

At last you come to the coast. A sleepy fishing village of simple wooden huts basks peacefully in the sun and you head towards it across a sandy beach, the sea rolling in to cool your tired feet. The sea is clear, blue and sparkling. A small and dingy single-sailed, three-man-crew fishing sloop is moored at a rickety wooden jetty. The crew are loading nets on board and a middle-aged man with blackened teeth and a weather-worn face is supervising them. His clothes are tattered and greasy. You hail him and they all turn in surprise and stare at you.

'Well, a stranger, by the gods', says the captain. 'And what do you want with poor fisher folk like us?' He speaks suspiciously, more than a trace of worry in his voice. 'Not more tribute for the Isle of Thieves I hope. We've nothing left.'

You reassure them that you come in peace, but this does not seem to assuage their fears. Knowing that nothing in the world would convince the captain to take you through the Fangs of Nadir, you offer to buy the boat from him. At this he brightens visibly, but refuses, saying that this is his livelihood and how could he feed his family on gold? You will have to persuade him to take you to one of the large cities on the Inner Sea, where you can purchase a boat.

You ask him to do so and he instantly agrees but he narrows his eye and regards you warily. 'How much you offerin'?' he grunts. Will you give 10 gold pieces (turn to **24**) or 20 (turn to **60**)?

3

After the debate concerning the army, the Privy Council does not resume session for a tenday, giving you time to assess how the changes you have ordered are affecting the city. If your Popularity Rating is zero or less turn to **315**. If not turn to **325**.

4

You hold up the Scorpion Ring as your words echo around the rock-enclosed clearing. There is a moment's silence and then a voice rings out, seemingly from nowhere, 'What, then, is the Word, Wielder of the Secret Shadow?' You curse mentally, for you do not know any password, nor the ritual of its saying.

Will you dive towards the nearest rock outcrop (turn to **406**) or say, 'I have no time for this; my mission is of the utmost importance to the Grandmaster and he wished for me to convey the news to him as quickly as possible! Let me pass or you will know his wrath!' (turn to **136**)?

5

The Demagogue is quite agitated; his voice changes pitch disconcertingly. 'The people are only reacting high-spiritedly to the good news of your coronation, Your Majesty. Is it not time for the common people to be allowed to be law-keepers themselves? The Watch are no more than a symbol of oppression. We must encourage men and women in the streets to report wrong-doings to the Palace instead.'

Turn back to **373**.

6

As he swings the sickle at you, you leap into the air and attempt to twist your legs about his head and throw him.

GRANDMASTER OF SHADOWS
Defence against Teeth of the Tiger throw: 7
Endurance: 15
Damage: 1 Die + 1

If you succeed, you send him cartwheeling to the ground. You land on your feet and as he jumps up you may kick him (turn to **30**) or punch him (turn to **18**) adding 2 to your Modifier and damage for this attack only. If you failed to throw him, he sweeps your legs aside with his left arm and as you land on your feet beside him he spins and drives the sickle at your back. Your Defence is 6. If you still live, will you execute a Forked Lightning kick (turn to **30**) or a Cobra Strike (turn to **18**)?

7

It is customary in most of the cities of the Manmarch to raise money through temple taxes. In this way some of the contributions of the people are channelled to the treasury. Later that day the Privy Councillors are in session once more to decide upon this issue of taxation. Whichever of the following are present – Parsifal, Force-Lady Gwyneth, the Lord High Steward, Solstice, Golspiel, the Demagogue and Greystaff – they place their clenched fists on the table, indicating that they wish to speak. Anyone present who does not do so, either has no advice to give or does not *wish* to give any. You may authorize any or all four of your Privy Councillors to speak in the following order:

Parsifal or Force-Lady Gwyneth: Turn to **19**.

The Lord High Steward: Turn to **37**.

Solstice: Turn to **183**.

Golspiel: Turn to **193**.

The Demagogue: Turn to **67**.

Greystaff: Turn to **77**.

When you have heard all or all you wish to hear, turn to **87**.

8

Your throwing star hurtles through the air to hit your target's back with a crack. The force of the blow sends the figure toppling forward. It crashes to the ground and shatters. You start in surprise as you realise it was only a clay dummy, a trick. Almost simultaneously a trapdoor opens in the ceiling and another black-garbed ninja, with a sai – an iron spike with two sharpened quillons – in each hand, drops down. However, the ninja hesitates for a moment, expecting you to be beside the dummy, and thus gives you time to dart forward. As he hisses in anger and turns to meet your attack, you drive a straight-fingered Cobra Strike at his throat. The Scorpion Ninja's Defence is 7. If you succeed, turn to **20**. If not, turn to **32**.

9

'By the gods, run!' someone yells and the crowd melts away like water. Looking up you can see scores of red and black scaled dragons in the sky. The sound of a hundred leathery wings beating the air washes over the city. The priests disappear back into the temple but the shining warriors surround their leader and his son. Paladin's face is grim as he looks up, 'Never have I seen so many at one time!' Then the dragons dive towards the city and the tower ballistae open fire. Volleys of enormous spear-like arrows speed heavenward, searing off dragon scales or sinking into soft underbellies. The priests of Rocheval appear at the towers and on the temple roofs; lancing bolts of white fire flash from their hands into the midst of the dragon hosts and some dragons plummet earthward to be caught in the nets.

'To your posts,' shouts Paladin, and his warriors run to the highest point of the city's turrets.

Then the dragons unleash a terrible assault on the city. Great spurts of flame burst from the mouths of the red dragons and rivers of acid erupt from the mouths of the black dragons. But, strangely, they ignore the towers and the ballistae, and concentrate on the nets. Even though the rope nets are coated in fire-resistant material, the massed flames and acid burn it away in huge sections.

Paladin is torn between shouting at his son to get into hiding and shouting orders to the city guardsmen. His son is resolutely refusing to leave, determined to fight at his father's side.

Several dragons have been slain, and suddenly they switch from the nets to the city defences and a terrible battle rages on. However, the nets have almost completely burned away. Then a bright blue speck high in the sky resolves itself into a truly enormous dragon, with iridescent blue scales. It drops out of the sky straight at Paladin and his son.

'Back,' he cries, pushing his son away, and he stands, legs apart, sword at the ready. Just before the massive blue dragon is about to hit the ground it whips out its wings and they fill the air with a crack. It hangs above Paladin, great eyes glaring in rage and anticipation. It speaks, its voice booming, resonant with evil. 'At last,' it says. Then a cracking bolt of lightning leaps from its jaws. It strikes Paladin's gleaming white sword, and there is an incandescent flash. He is hurled through the air to crash in a heap. Slowly and groggily he battles to lift himself up – he is but stunned. The boy shouts out, 'No!' and dashes towards the dragon, shortsword in hand – obviously no match for the enormous monster. Will you decide this affair is none of your business, head to the quayside and take a boat in all the commotion (turn to **402**) or run forward to try to save the young boy (turn to **84**)?

10

The Mountains of Undying Solitude loom before you, dark and forbidding, like gnarled fingers clawing blindly at the dirty grey sky. A cold biting wind that chills your bones strikes up as you move through the foothills. The black clouds, heavy and ponderous, empty themselves on the lifeless earth and great sheets of freezing rain and sleet buffet you as you struggle upward. It is as if the mountains themselves were trying to sweep you off their sides, just as a man would remove an insect that troubled him. The land is all but barren, a hostile land tortured by the elements, where few plants or animals, let alone men, can survive.

As you climb, you come to some sparse vegetation, shrubs and bushes, blowing violently in the keening wind as if they struggled desperately against something that sought to tear them by the roots from the life-giving earth. A mountain goat huddles miserably under a small bush, looking at you dumbly as you pass by. Water runs off your body in rivulets and it is not long before you are struggling upwards through a small rushing torrent as the rain cascades down the mountainside. It is only your rigorous training that enables you to withstand this punishing weather.

You clamber on, fatigue creeping up on you slowly. Eventually, you come to a halt. A great chasm opens up before you as if some god-like Titan had slashed the earth with his sword. Beyond it, and rising up into the sky, are the Crags of Abandoned Hope, crooked jumbles of stone, towering upward above the mountain like a crown. A thin stone bridge, about two feet wide, spans the chasm – of natural origin, not man-made. Up above you the mountain leans over and joins the massive expanse of forbidding stone on the other side. A difficult climb, but you could reach the other side by climbing up and across, and then onward to the crags. Will you cross the thin bridge (turn to **22**) or, if you have the skill of Climbing, go upwards and across (turn to **34**)?

11

You had been warned of this. You look grimly down at Mandrake, recognisable now that he is making no effort to mimic the High Grandmaster. Here in the confessional room you bring swift death to the assassin. Before he can recover from your stunning attack you finish him off with a chop to the neck. Your reactions have not suffered even though you have been relying more on your wits than your body of late.

Mandrake's disguise was perfect. He had killed Parsifal two days before, having already spent some days watching him in secret. He got to know the routine of the temple, and even those closest to the High Grandmaster had been unable to spot him for an imposter. He had even met and talked with Force-Lady Gwyneth about the Order of the Yellow Lotus without arousing her suspicions. He was a formidable foe but you have triumphed again, the first ever to survive the attentions of the Guildmaster of Assassins. You order the monks to select a new High Grandmaster and lead the prayer of thanksgiving for the life and works of Parsifal yourself.

Without Foxglove's help you might well be dead and you send her a message of thanks. Tomorrow there will be a banquet to celebrate your survival. Turn to **162**.

12

You head east into the mountains. After a long and arduous climb through the cold inhospitable Mountains of Undying Solitude you begin the descent on the other side. Eventually you have arrived at the foothills. You travel on, trotting constantly for miles across the barren wilderness, until you come to more fertile lands. A faint smell of the sea comes to your nostrils and you head towards it, knowing you must find transport across the Inner Sea. The journey takes several days and passes uneventfully.

At last you come to the coast. Standing on a hillock you survey a long sandy beach. The sea, clear and blue, sparkles in the sun, and the air is fresh with the tang of salt water. You notice a small single-sailed boat, pulled up on the beach a few hundred yards away, and you walk over to it. There is nobody nearby; but a fishing net, a tarpaulin and some old oilskins are stacked neatly on the beach. You leave 15 gold pieces on the tarpaulin and push the boat out to sea and leap in. You find a few days' rations inside it. Soon you are sailing across the Inner Sea. A fair wind is behind you and perilous adventure ahead; your spirit soars. The weather is good and you sail on for two days, a restful and uneventful journey. You may restore up to 8 points of lost Endurance.

Eventually, an island appears ahead. When you are closer you can see it has a city-port, whose white walls glow redly in the setting sun. According to your map it should be Haven of Tor. Will you put in at the port (turn to **102**) or sail east toward the Fangs of Nadir (turn to **79**)?

13

The selection of your Privy Councillors is complete. The other four seats beside your own in Star Chamber are filled and it is time for you to take your place at the head of the table. The servants and courtiers disperse as you stride quickly towards Star Chamber. The rheumy old eyes of Parsifal, High Grandmaster of the Temple to Kwon, follow you reproachfully. Turn to **163.**

14

As you jump forward the Unicorn snorts and whinnies, darting away into the forest like an arrow, its eyes regarding you disdainfully as it goes. You were nowhere near to reaching it. Shrugging your shoulders, you press on through the forest. A day and a night pass uneventfully – it is as if the forest inhabitants are avoiding you, even though you move with the stealth of a panther. You rest well in any case, and you may restore 3 points of lost Endurance.

At last you emerge from the forest to stand on the shores of the Elemental Sea. A small island lies more than half a mile out to sea and you guess this to be the one the Grandmaster of Shadows spoke of. You are a strong swimmer and the distance would be easy for you normally, but between you and the island rages the Elemental Sea. It seems calm enough save where sudden geysers and spouts of water erupt randomly and whirl along at enormous speed for a little way, back and forth, raging like a wall of water, before subsiding into the sea once more. It is aptly named, for these are Water Elementals. Taking a deep breath and sending a prayer to Kwon, you dive into the water and strike out for the island.

Make a Fate Roll. If Fate smiles on you, turn to **54**. If Fate turns her back on you, turn to **74**.

15

Whose advice will you act on? Will you follow the ideas of Parsifal or Gwyneth (turn to **25**), Golspiel (turn to **35**), the Lord High Steward (turn to **45**) or the Demagogue (turn to **55**)?

16

You hold up the Scorpion Ring and your words echo around the rock-enclosed clearing. There is a moment's silence. Then a figure drops down from above, a fall of twenty feet, to land nimbly before you barely making a sound. He stands legs apart, facing you, hands at his sides. It is a ninja of the Way of the Scorpion, dressed in black from head to toe, and with a short curved sword strapped to his back. He says nothing but steps aside and points up the rock-face that leads to the base of the crags, signalling you to go on, his eyes regarding you inscrutably from the thin slit of his hood.

If you have the skill of ShinRen, turn to **88**.

If you have not, will you walk past the ninja and climb the rock-face (turn to **100**) or immediately attack him (turn to **112**)?

17

When the Palace crier proclaims that Golspiel has been appointed Guildmaster of Merchants he is pelted with eggs and rotten fruit and as he leaves the Palace he is forced to abandon dignity and scuttle back inside the confines of the Palace garden. The news is greeted by the people as a sign that you are bound to the hated Golspiel because of his wealth. They also realise that the price of bread and everything else is bound to rise. Subtract 1 from your Popularity Rating and turn to **7**.

He swings his sickle in an arc from left to right. You intercept his forearm with your arm and step in, driving a straight-fingered jab into his side, under the rib cage. If you succeed and you have the skill of Yubi-Jutsu, you may add 1 to the damage.

GRANDMASTER OF SHADOWS
Defence against Cobra Strike punch: 7
Endurance: 15
Damage: 1 Die + 1

If you have defeated him, turn to **42**. If not, he drops down and tries to hook the sickle behind your knee and hamstring you. Your Defence is 7 as you flip backwards in an attempt to avoid his attack. If you survive, will you try a Forked Lightning kick (turn to **30**), a Teeth of the Tiger throw (turn to **6**) or another Cobra Strike (return to the top of this paragraph)?

The High Grandmaster – Parsifal – and Force-Lady Gwyneth have obviously come to an agreement about the correct course for you to take. If either is not a Councillor then the two stand on the platform below the oval table from which those who are not Privy Councillors may address Star Chamber. They stand side by side, he a shade shorter than she and wearing his monk's habit; she as martial as ever, wearing a surcoat with the diamond shield blazen of Dama on top of worn chain-mail. It is Parsifal who addresses the Council: 'Majesty, tradition says that each of the five major Temples be taxed equally but for many years we have had to pay crippling taxes, whilst the Temple to Time paid none, and priests of Nemesis grew fat on the proceeds. We suggest, Your Majesty, that you fine the Temple to Nemesis five talents and levy a tax of one talent from the Temple to Time. When next you need taxes we may then return to the old system of equal tithing. In this way, Overlord, you may win the hearts of the people by undoing some of the wrongs done by the Usurper.'

Gwyneth adds, 'The people feel that the priests of Nemesis have escaped lightly under your rule. Punish them Overlord.'

Turn back to 7.

20

He tries to block your hand but fails. The blow smashes into his windpipe with such force that it crumples inward. Dropping the two sai, he staggers back, gurgling and choking, struggling for breath. You follow up with a devastating Forked Lightning kick to his stomach and head, thus finishing off your opponent, who falls inert. Turn to 44.

21

The Orcs were brought as slaves from the Purple Mountains to the City of Irsmuncast three hundred years ago. Their families were given citizenship a century later. Your proclamation banishing both them and the mixed-blooded Halvorcs swings the general mood against you. The people become fed up; you are a tyrant to them, no different from the Usurper. They lose their confidence in your ability to rule wisely. Agitators whip up feeling against you and scrolls accusing you of weakness, injustice, favouritism, treachery to the people, and a list of other criticisms almost without end, circulate the city. You are reading one of these scandal-mongering rags when the priests of Nemesis come for you. Nobody will lift a finger to save you. After a valiant struggle, your bodyguards are killed and you are taken to be broken on the wheel in view of the Temple to Kwon. Evil rules once more in the City of Irsmuncast nigh Edge.

22

You walk out onto the sliver of rock. The wind is stronger here, howling up the chasm like a banshee, threatening to pluck you from the stone and dash you to the floor of the chasm like so much balsa wood. Grimly, you crouch down and cling to the rock, edging your way across. Down below,

darkness yawns. Then you notice a net, like a huge hammock, strung out below the bridge, as if to catch anything that falls off it. You are puzzling over what its purpose could be, here in this lonely place, when a great booming laugh rings out, echoing around the chasm yet almost drowned out by the screaming wind. At the other side stands a giant figure, ten feet tall. It is human in shape, dressed in goat hides, with huge arms and legs knotted with muscle and thick with hair. A single eye glares evilly at you from a horned, misshapen head. It is a Horned Cyclops and it holds a large rock in its hand. Several more lie at its feet.

'Well met, man-thing,' it roars. 'You shall make a pleasant change from goat meat!'

It hurls a rock at you in an attempt to knock you off the bridge into the net. You just manage to duck the massive stone, but any pronounced movements cause you to teeter dangerously as the wind is strong and your footing precarious. The beast is hefting another rock. Will you scramble in an attempt to reach the other side as quickly as possible (turn to **46**) or inch forward slowly and attempt to avoid any rocks (turn to **58**)?

23

When the doors are swept open again, a man with a white skull-cap and voluminous white robes walks into the Throne Room. It is Greystaff, High Priest of the Temple to Avatar. He has a kindly, though solemn, face and is thin and a little pallid for want of the sun. There is an aura of saintliness about him as well which arrests your attention. If you have the skill of ShinRen, the Training of the Heart, turn to **43**. If not read on:

Greystaff bows low and says, 'Avatar be praised for granting us deliverance at your hands, Great Majesty. The taint of evil has poisoned the sewers of this troubled city for too long. I would like to help you expunge the taint that the rule of the Dark Usurper has left in all our hearts, to show people how to walk with uplifted hearts and heads. As you know we who worship Avatar prize goodness above all things, and the great sage, Veritégal, once wrote that every

Overlord should have at least one soul of goodly persuasion as his adviser. I humbly profess that in all my thoughts and deeds I strive to be this. I await your decision, Great Majesty.'

Will you ask Greystaff to step into Star Chamber (turn to **53**) or disappoint him (turn to **63**)?

24

He grunts and says, 'I'll take you as far as the Isle of Thieves for that and no further! Get in. We're ready to cast off in any case.' You will have to try and purchase a boat there.

A few hours later, you are scudding across a deep blue sea in perfect weather, a fair wind behind you and perilous adventure ahead. Your spirits soar and you send a joyful prayer of faith to Kwon.

Two days pass and you may restore another 3 points of lost Endurance. On the third day the Captain, who has ignored you up to now, says, 'We shall arrive at the island tomorrow.'

Will you ask him where you could find an Amulet of Nullaq (turn to **72**) or thank him and say nothing (turn to **86**)?

25

Force-Lady Gwyneth heads the Watch to good effect. The sight of the shieldmaidens patrolling on horseback, two-by-two, restores calm to the city. The impartiality shown when she and her troops bring wrongdoers to justice wins you instant popularity, so add 1 to your Popularity Rating. Over the tenday you will see that Gwyneth is able to carry out a difficult job well and Irsmuncast is to become one of the safer cities in the Manmarch. The Force-Lady will undertake to bear the large costs involved in paying the shieldmaidens' wages from her temple's funds if you will exempt the Pyramid Temple from temple tax. You agree gladly since the treasury's coffers are empty. Note that you cannot follow the advice of anyone suggesting a tax on the Temple to Dama, note these Keepers of the Watch on the Charter of Rulership, and turn to **353**.

26

The forest is murky and dark, musty with the smell of ages. After a few hours' travel you encounter a stream and decide to follow it. Beams of sunlight penetrate the darkness ahead and moments later you are standing at the edge of a clearing through which the stream runs. A fabulous beast of great beauty and presence is drinking gracefully from the stream and you stand awe-struck for a time. It is a Unicorn. Its silvery flanks almost seem to gleam like armour and its golden horn spirals delicately upward. Great are the powers of the Unicorn's horn and most fortunate is he who can master the Unicorn as his steed. Will you run forward and try to leap onto the Unicorn's back (turn to **14**) or stay where you are and do nothing (turn to **36**)?

27

For all his smooth veneer the gross merchant quickly becomes livid with barely-suppressed rage, his face turning a dangerous shade of puce. For a short time he is at a loss for words.

If his mercenaries, led by Antocidas the One-Eyed, are Keepers of the Watch turn to **57**.

If not, he mutters bitterly that your father, who always kept his promises, was more honourable than you; then he shuffles out, leaving the odour of sweet hair oil behind him. Turn to **7**.

28

Seemingly from nowhere, a thin sliver of steel comes whirring toward you. You recognise it as a shuriken, but not of the kind you are accustomed to. Almost by instinct, you whip your forearm up and sweep the deadly missile aside. It whirrs shrilly as it strikes your iron sleeves and then clatters against the rock-face. A clipped shout fills the air and a figure dressed as you leaps down from above, a twenty-foot fall, to land nimbly before you. As the ninja, for that is what he is, hits the ground he reaches behind his back and draws the short curved sword that lies there. 'You are not of the Scorpion,' he whispers. 'Prepare to die,' and he somersaults forward, to come up slashing at your legs. Nimbly, you leap above the flashing blade and launch an attack of your own. Will you try to slide under his guard and execute a Dragon's Tail throw (turn to **52**), try a Winged Horse kick (turn to **64**) or try to close in and drive a Cobra Strike up at his throat (turn to **76**)?

29

You rear back in terror, but the Kraken, a daughter of Nullaq, seems to respond to the magical, and evil, aura of the Amulet. Its tentacles cease to writhe and the hideous monstrosity sinks down, quiescent. Slowly it disappears, back into the watery depths. Spluttering, you swim on. Then a great geyser erupts beside you, and another Elemental rises up like a liquid tornado. Quickly, you dive down in an attempt to swim under it. Make another Fate Roll, but subtract 2 from your Fate Modifier for this roll. If Fate is with you, turn to **246**. If Fate is against you, turn to **258**.

30

The Grandmaster swings the sickle down at the side of your neck, but you take the shaft in the palm of your outstretched hand and then drive a kick at his knee and up again at his head. If you succeed and you have the skill of Yubi-Jutsu, you may add 1 to the damage.

GRANDMASTER OF SHADOWS
Defence against Forked Lightning kick: 7
Endurance: 15
Damage: 1 Die + 1

If you have beaten him, turn to **42**. If not, he swings the sickle up in a backhand strike aimed at your midriff. Your Defence is 7 as you hop back onto your toes and try to drive both your hands down onto his wrist. If you survive, will you try a Cobra Strike punch (turn to **18**), a Teeth of the Tiger throw (turn to **6**) or another Forked Lightning kick (return to the top of this paragraph)?

The Usurper's Lord High Steward sweeps into the room like a great blackhawk. His silver and sable cloak is topped by curving wings of black velvet at the shoulders. His face is pale and drawn with a long thin nose and a little grey goatee which emphasises the length and point of his chin. He bows elaborately and says, 'Your Majesty, I have been running this city since the death of your father. In that time we have suffered no attack from beyond the city walls. I know more about the problems of this city, its religions and races than any other. I am practised in statecraft and I am the representative of the Temple to Nemesis, without whose support your days as Overlord will be numbered. I give you my word that I will act in your best interest and not seek to supplant you. Our people deserve to be represented on the Privy Council like any other. And so I believe you must appoint me to Star Chamber.'

He seems about to go on but checks himself. There is no missing the veiled threat in his manner. About three in ten of the beings in Irsmuncast worship Nemesis, the Supreme Principle of Evil. You must decide between pleasing them and the usefulness of the Steward and the potential danger of adding to his power. If you order the Lord High Steward into Star Chamber turn to **51**. If, instead, you disappoint him turn to **61**.

32

He twists his left arm up and across, knocking your jab aside and thrusting at your left thigh at the same time. He is fighting in close quarters and he cannot get much force behind the blow. However, the pain is real enough. Lose 2 Endurance. If you still live, you pull your left leg back and stamp your other foot at the inside of his extended right knee. The bone snaps with a crack and the ninja cries out in pain as he staggers back. You follow it up with three rapid punches, an Iron Fist to the stomach, a Cobra Strike at his eyes and a Tiger's Paw to the side of his neck. He collapses, pole-axed. Turn to **44**.

33

You pass through an archway in the wall of the lowest tier. A wide staircase, clear and bright in the sun, stretches up to the topmost galleries, where you can make out several temples, gleaming in the sun. Many people seem to be heading up so you decide to see what is attracting them. After a tiring walk you step through another archway to a lovely sight. Several temples – buildings of breathtaking architectural beauty – border a wide-open courtyard of flat marble. You recognise temples, to Time, the All-Mother, Gauss and Illustra (the Fountain of Love) but the largest and most awesome is the fortress-like Temple to Rocheval, the Prince of Knights Errant and wielder of the Holy of Holies. A great crowd of townsfolk has massed at the edge of the courtyard, waiting expectantly.

Then a troop of people emerges from the Temple to Rocheval. A line of white-robed priests is flanked by a line of warriors dressed in shining armour, great red crosses embroidered upon their surcoats. Each and every one seems to radiate an aura of purity.

But it is the towering warrior at the head of the procession that draws gasps from the crowds, especially amongst the women. He is tall and strong, bearing an unsheathed great sword across his back that pulses with white light. Such presence you have never before seen. You have to resist the temptation to kneel before him and swear

lifelong fealty to this god-like warrior. His eyes are a striking steel grey and he seems to radiate peace and goodwill.

'Paladin, it is Paladin,' the crowd murmurs, 'Keeper of the Holy Order of the Errants Templar.'

At Paladin's side walks a young man, no more than fourteen summers, obviously his son. You guess this to be a ceremony of his coming of age. Suddenly a great horn blast fills the air, echoing around the courtyard. A cry goes up, 'Dragon Attack, Dragon Attack.'

Turn to **9**.

34

You tie the cat's claws to your hands and feet, and swing the grappling hook up high. It clatters against the stone, barely audible over the rushing wind, and anchors itself on an outcrop of rock. You haul your weather-beaten body upwards, crawling like a fly up the sheer rock-face, hands and feet finding holds where no ordinary human could. Just as you feel that your aching limbs will not serve your will any longer, you reach the top.

Down below, the thin stone bridge spans the chasm like a tightrope. Below that, yawning blackness. A gnarled mass of stone arcs downwards to the other side. Beyond it a mountain track leads upwards towards the Crags of Abandoned Hope that reach skyward; higher still, you notice a cave mouth near the track, but it is the creature emerging from the cave that holds your attention. A massive humanoid figure lumbers out, sniffing the air, as if it had caught the scent of prey – presumably you. Its knotted limbs are heavy with muscle and hair. A single eye stares out from a misshapen head, topped by a wicked-looking horn. It is a Horned Cyclops. It descends the pathway to the chasm's edge looking intently across the bridge, obviously expecting to see something upon it. When it finds nothing it looks about suspiciously but does not spot you. Will you descend and attack the creature from above (turn to **382**) or climb down to the path behind it and head on up to the crags in an attempt to avoid it (turn to **370**)?

35

You thank Golspiel warmly. Financing and equipping the Watch for a city the size of Irsmuncast is a costly business. Golspiel is clearly a very wealthy man. Antocidas the One-Eyed and his mercenaries certainly seem capable of deterring any open hostility to your rule but they also provoke a certain amount of resentment with their high-handed justice. Tales of bribery and corruption will begin filtering back to you over the tenday that follows and it will seem that some of the money the rich are paying, to avoid being arrested on trumped-up charges, might be finding its way into a corrupt Golspiel's vast coffers. The mercenaries are to become hated by most of the people and you will be forced to depend on them heavily for protection. Note these Keepers of the Watch on the Charter of Rulership and subtract 2 from your Popularity Rating. Turn to **353**.

36

The Unicorn finishes drinking and canters away into the forest, a vision of grace and beauty. Then a figure steps out from behind a tree, dressed in oak-leaf green, an ash bow in one hand. It is a Wood Elf, with chestnut brown hair and amber eyes. He speaks in a rich and melodious voice, 'Welcome, stranger, to the Forest of Fables. I am glad you did not try to harm our brother, the Unicorn. My name is Galanwiel, and I am the lord of the Elves of the forest.' Several more Elves, dressed as he, step out as if from nowhere. They have obviously been following you – not even your heightened sense of woodcraft was able to detect their presence.

If you are an Elf-Friend, turn to **132**. If Paladin of Haven of Tor gave you a Gold Signet Ring, turn to **174**. If neither of these apply, turn to **108**.

37

The Lord High Steward smiles for once before beginning his speech, but the facial expression produced is so at variance with his cold stiff bearing that the desired effect is lost. 'There are those within the city who say that we priests of

Nemesis have grown fat on the taxes of other temples. It is not true. The Usurper took all and spent like a prodigal son. Money disappeared into the treasury coffers and was never seen again. We are ready to pay our equal tithe of tax in common with the other temples to Time, Dama, Avatar and Kwon – a talent from each temple. This will raise five talents of gold for the treasury. It also represents a fair basis for taxation which will not prove unpopular.' He sits down and looks at his fellow Councillors from under hooded lids. Turn back to **7**.

38

A stretch of coastline appears to the south-east. You can see a storm brewing on the horizon, but there is little you can do about it, in your little boat. Quickly, you furl the sail. A few long hours later you are beset by buffeting winds and crashing waves, and your boat is tossed about willy-nilly. Day has turned to night, as heavy black clouds blot out the sun, and torrential rain begins to fill your boat faster than you can bail it out. Finally, the little boat is thrown up by a huge wave and you are hurled into the raging sea. It is all you can do to keep your head above water and you struggle on for many hours. Only your powers of endurance save you from drowning.

Exhausted and half conscious, you are eventually washed up on a sandy beach. You lie there for an interminable period of time, too tired to move. When you have regained some strength, you look up to see a thick wall of vegetation stretching away to either side, a dense forest. Taking out your sodden map you guess it to be the Forest of Fables. If you head north-east, you should come out on the shore of the Elemental Sea and thus avoid the Fangs of Nadir completely, although even your heart quails at the thought of swimming across the Elemental Sea, for it is said to be impossibly perilous, even without a Kraken inhabiting its depths. But you will have to cross that bridge when you come to it. Picking yourself up, you enter the dense forest.

Turn to **26**.

39

There is a strange spluttering and fizzing sound underneath the oval table and then the whole chamber fills suddenly with smoke. The other Privy Councillors collapse to the floor but you are off your throne and out before the noisome fumes can affect you. You slam the doors shut. To your horror one of your bodyguards kills her sister-at-arms, decapitating the shieldmaiden even as you watch. Then the doors are flung open and Parsifal, clutching a wet handkerchief to his face staggers out into the Throne Room. Will you ignore him and kill the shieldmaiden who is preparing to attack you (turn to **279**) or knock Parsifal to the floor using the Dragon's Tail throw (turn to **289**)?

40

Seemingly from nowhere a thin sliver of steel comes whirring towards you. You recognise it as a shuriken, but not of the kind you are accustomed to. Before you can act, it buries itself in your thigh, and you wince in pain. Lose 4 Endurance. If you are still alive, you pluck it out and throw it aside – at least it was not poisoned. A clipped shout fills the air and a figure dressed as you leaps down from above, a twenty foot fall, to land nimbly before you. As the ninja, for that is what he is, hits the ground he reaches behind his back and draws the short curved sword that lies there. 'You are not of the Scorpion,' he whispers. 'Prepare to die,' and he somersaults forward, to come up slashing at your legs. Nimbly, you leap above the flashing blade and launch an attack of your own. Will you try to slide under his guard and execute a Dragon's Tail throw (turn to **52**), try a Winged Horse kick (turn to **64**) or try to close in and drive a Cobra Strike up at his throat (turn to **76**)?

41

Parsifal beckons and a young page boy hands him a scroll from which he begins to read as you look over his shoulder.

'First Supplicant: the Lord High Steward of the Usurper's court, a follower of Nemesis who administered the city at the whim of the Dark Overlord.

'Second Supplicant: Force-Lady Gwyneth, High Priestess of the Temple to Dama.

'Third Supplicant: Golspiel of the Silver Tongue, a merchant.

'Fourth Supplicant: the Demagogue, a mob orator, popular with the common people.

'Fifth Supplicant: Greystaff, High Priest of the Temple to Avatar.

'Sixth Supplicant: Foxglove, a priestess of Nemesis, the head of the Usurper's 'secret informers' – a master spy.

'Seventh Supplicant: Solstice, High Priest of the Temple to Time.

'Eighth Supplicant: Parsifal, High Grandmaster of the Temple to Kwon — my humble self, Your Majesty.'

You can order the page to show you the scroll of supplicants again at any time. Note this paragraph number down so that you can refer to the scroll if you should need to do so, but remember also the paragraph you are reading at the time.

As you enter the Throne Room, all those present kneel. Parsifal bows and backs out into the vestibule. Though he is High Grandmaster he shows every mark of respect. A hush descends as the first supplicant walks into the room.

Turn to **31**.

42

Your last blow knocks him backwards and he falls to sprawl on his back at your feet. He tries to rise but the effort is too much for him and his head crashes back to the ground. He groans, barely breathing. Then he lifts his head and points at you with one hand, his arm crooked. He rasps, in a voice cracked with pain, 'You have done well, Avenger. You are a great ninja. But I'm afraid you have wasted your time after all,' and he smiles weakly. 'I shall die, but you shall not find the Orb and Sceptre here! They lie beyond the Fangs of Nadir, the dashing rocks of the Inner Sea,' and he laughs, but is cut short by a spasm of pain. A trickle of blood runs from his lips as he struggles to speak on. 'Beyond the Fangs, a Kraken waits to devour all those who approach the Jaws of

Forgetfulness. Only the bearer of an Amulet of Nullaq will it not devour! An island lies near the centre of the Elemental Sea. Upon that island lies the Orb and Sceptre of Telmain I, long-dead ruler of Irsmuncast. But –' he pauses for breath, 'a Devil-Beast guards them... Your task has but begun, Avenger.'

You know a Devil-Beast to be a demonic thing created by the priests of Death, from the dead body of an Elf, an abomination to Elves. Suddenly the dying Grandmaster straightens his arm and flicks his wrist. There is a click and a thin sliver of steel flies forth, catching you completely unawares. It buries itself in your left eye, putting it out instantly. You throw your hands to your face and cry out. Dragging it out brings a rush of blood. The Grandmaster gives a last sigh and slumps back, dead, as you staunch the flow of blood from your wound. All that is left is a gaping hole. Your Punch, Kick, and Throw Modifiers are reduced by 1 until you can find some way of restoring sight to your left eye. You twist your hood so that it covers the unseemly sight of your ruined eye.

Hopping over the body, you examine the altar. The idol of Nemesis seems to regard you malevolently. You find a secret cache inside, containing two potions, one easily identifiable as poison, the other a Potion of Healing, which you may drink at any time when you are not in combat to restore up to 10 points of lost Endurance (note it on your Character Sheet). There is also a small chest of gold coins, about a few dozen, and several gems which you decide may be useful, although you find it completely incomprehensible that many find the sparkling, coloured stones so fascinating.

As you are walking to the stairs, several ninja file into the room, to stand in two rows flanking the exit. You step back in dismay – you feel too tired. But one of them says, 'You have penetrated to the centre of our most secret and well-guarded place and slain our Grandmaster. Because of this, we are honour-bound to let you go free, much as it irks us. You have performed a great deed and we will not hinder your passage,' and they step aside. As you ascend the vortex-shaped stairs, he continues, 'But for the killing of our

Grandmaster and the dishonour you have heaped upon us, your life is forfeit. This debt of honour shall be settled. May Nemesis devour your soul!'

Some time later, you are above ground. It is morning now and the sun shines brightly on the idyllic valley that hides the evil cult of assassins in its bones. You will have to cross the Inner Sea to reach the Fangs of Nadir. Examine your map. Will you cross the mountains to the east to the shore of the Inner Sea (turn to **12**) or cross the mountains to the west reaching the shore that way (turn to **2**)?

43

Of all the people you have so far considered for the role of Privy Councillor, Greystaff is the most artless. He radiates goodness and is possessed of great strength of will. He is far from confident you will choose him, however, perhaps because he is not the head of one of the more powerful temples. Turn back to **23** and read on.

44

Stepping over the body, you approach the door ahead of you. It is studded with many bolts, shaped like scorpions. An enormous whirlpool symbol is painted upon it. The handle turns easily and you open it a fraction and step through in one fluid motion, ready for action, into another corridor. In the dim light, you come face to face with another ninja – this one is unarmed, the same height and build as you, tensed and ready for action. The ninja's costume is tattered and torn in places, as if from constant battle, and the eyes seem to glitter with determined resolve. This ninja has an almost tangible aura of power and strength. Will you unleash a flying Winged Horse kick (turn to **56**) or step back into a defensive posture (turn to **68**)?

The Lord High Steward stalks out of Star Chamber to make arrangements for reconstituting the Usurper's Watch, tactfully passing over some of the most hated officers. His tactics are effective but the city seems to go into a state of shock when it realises that after the revolution the followers of Nemesis are still able to oppress. You let it be known that the Lord High Steward is accountable to you and he, at least in public, acknowledges this but you are to witness demonstrations and stone-throwing beginning a few days later. Note the Temple to Nemesis as Keepers of the Watch on the Charter of Rulership and subtract 2 from your Popularity Rating. Turn to **353**.

You scramble forward in a low crouch, the wind plucking at your clothes. Make a Fate Roll. If Fate smiles on you, turn to **82**. If Fate turns her back on you, turn to **94**.

Faster than sight, your sleeve-guard whips across shattering the fragile blade. You follow up with a blinding flurry of attacks, killing the Guildmaster of Assassins outright. Your reactions have not suffered even though you have been relying on your wits rather than your body of late. Tomorrow there will be a banquet to celebrate your survival. Turn to **419**.

The swan-prowed boat glides forward at a word, angling closer to the left-hand rock. The water is a broiling maelstrom but the boat sails on. You grip its sides as it tries to hold its course through the heaving waters. The noise is deafening as the elvan boat bucks and shudders through the Fangs of Nadir. Suddenly the sea boils upwards as the rocks begin to close again – you think you are about to be crushed when the boat surges forward into calmer waters. The rocks come together behind you with a great crash. Heaving a sigh of relief, you look out onto the Elemental Sea. A small island lies not more than half a mile away from you, but between you and it rages the Elemental Sea. You guess it to be the one the Grandmaster of Shadows spoke of. It seems calm enough save where sudden geysers and spouts of water erupt randomly and whirl along at enormous speed for a little way, back and forth, ranging around like a wall of water, before subsiding into the sea once more. It is aptly named, for these are Water Elementals.

You command the boat onward, praying to Kwon that an Elemental will not surge up below you. However, much to your surprise and joy, the elvan boat seems to sense the presence of these liquid creatures and is obviously able to avoid them, for it weaves and dodges its way to the island and somehow manages to avoid them as they fountain up around you, playing joyfully it seems. The island is drawing closer when there is a sudden boiling of the water before you, on a much greater scale than that caused by the Water Elementals. Huge tentacles clear the wave-tops and begin wildly thrashing the sea, and a great bloated squid-like body heaves itself up, water cascading off it in torrential rivulets. Two milky eyes stare at you balefully – the eyes of the Kraken. A great beaked maw clashes before you, as you struggle to stay afloat in the tumult of its rising. If you have an Amulet of Nullaq, turn to **138**. If not, turn to **186**.

49

There is a strange spluttering and fizzing sound underneath the oval table and then the whole chamber fills suddenly with smoke. The other Privy Councillors collapse to the floor but you are off your throne and out through the double doors before the noisome fumes can affect you. You slam the doors shut and the two monks of Kwon who form your bodyguard close in on either side of you. Suddenly, the doors are flung open and Parsifal, clutching a wet handkerchief to his face, staggers out into the Throne Room. Will you rush to him to see if he needs help or healing (turn to **229**) or up-end him using the Dragon's Tail throw (turn to **299**)?

50

You step in close and drive your fist at one of the eunuchs' flabby stomachs.

	1st BODYGUARD	2nd BODYGUARD
Defence against		
Iron Fist punch:	6	7
Endurance:	9	8
Damage:	1 Die + 2	1 Die + 2

If you have defeated them both, turn to **78**. If, not, your Defence is 6 if both are alive, and you may block only one attack. If only one is left, your Defence is 8. If you survive, will you try a Dragon's Tail throw (turn to **114**), a Leaping Tiger kick (turn to **66**) or another Iron Fist punch (return to the top of this paragraph)?

Note on your Charter of Rulership that the Lord High Steward is one of your Councillors. The Steward bows once more and sweeps majestically into Star Chamber. There are murmurings of disquiet all around and no-one will meet your eye. Turn to **71**.

He lunges at your neck but you have already hit the floor, your feet sliding at his. If this is the second or subsequent time you have tried to throw him, his Defence will be 8, not 7. This is noted by the slash under Defence.

NINJA SENTINEL
Defence against Dragon's Tail throw: 7/8
Endurance: 13
Damage: 1 Die + 1

If you succeed, you hook your legs around his and twist your body, tripping him. As agile as a cat you flip onto your feet just as your opponent rises. You decide to deliver a quick Cobra Strike as he is only slightly off balance (turn to **76**). You may add 2 to your Punch Modifier and damage for this attack only. If you fail to throw him, he hops backwards and then cuts down at your head as you leap up. Your Defence is 7, as you try to dodge aside. If you still live, will you try a Cobra Strike punch (turn to **76**) or a Winged Horse kick (turn to **64**)?

Greystaff bows and thanks you, then walks humbly into Star Chamber. Note that he is now one of your Privy Councillors on your Charter of Rulership. If you have already appointed four Councillors turn to **13**. If not turn to **73**.

Somehow you manage to avoid the Elementals that fountain up around you, playing joyfully, it seems. The island is drawing closer when there is a sudden boiling of the water before you, on a much greater scale than that caused by the Water Elementals. Huge tentacles suddenly clear the wave tops and begin wildly threshing the sea, and a great bloated squid-like body heaves itself up, water cascading off it in torrential rivulets. Two milky eyes stare at you balefully, the eyes of the Kraken. A great beaked maw clashes before you and its tentacles reach out to you, as you struggle to stay afloat in the tumult of its rising.

If you have an Amulet of Nullaq, turn to **29**. If not, turn to **204**.

55

The Demagogue spreads the word that the city is to be without a Watch. The people will be free from oppression if only they treat each other honestly and fairly. From a discreet position behind the windows of the royal balcony you watch the Demagogue's impassioned appeal to stop the looting which he makes from the Palace crier's podium in the centre of Palace Road. The looting continues into the night and the Demagogue stays up, walking the streets, appealing to the dignity of the people; the morning sun warms a tranquil city. Your move to let the Demagogue organise a Watch drawing on the common people is popular but misguided. Add 1 to your Popularity Rating.

Public order is not what it might be and you cannot justify convening Star Chamber for other matters. The Halls of Justice stand disused. After a few weeks, reports come in that followers of Vagar the Deceiver, thieves and vagabonds, are journeying north from Greyguilds-on-the-Moor to take rich pickings. It is soon unsafe to walk the streets at night. After a few tendays, order collapses and widespread looting occurs on the poorer Edgeside of the city. You are forced to form a new Watch. Turn back to **373** and take the advice of another of your Councillors. If no other is present as a member of the Council you may call any others mentioned at the beginning of **373** (excepting those who are imprisoned or dead) into Star Chamber *on this occasion only* and listen to their advice.

56

Lunging forward you drive your foot at the other ninja. It appears your opponent is doing the same but you are committed now. Your foot strikes home and suddenly the figure disappears with a splintering crash, appearing to dissolve before your eyes into shards of glittering light. You have just shattered a mirror you realise, as you land nimbly on your feet. But another figure stands behind the mirror, and you are too surprised to act for the moment. It is a gaunt, pale man in black robes adorned with whirlpool symbols, recognisable as a priest of Nemesis; he has a chain-mace at his side.

'Only a fool would seek to enter this den of Scorpions and expect to live, Avenger, you mindless lackey of that weak-willed so-called god of yours! May Nemesis, the Lord of Cleansing Flame, devour your soul,' and he gestures with his hands, mumbling some black incantation.

You double up in pain as an old wound re-opens, torn asunder by the power of the priest's magic. Lose 4 Endurance. If you still live, anger fills you and you prepare to attack. The priest's eyes widen in fear as he sees you still live; desperately he gestures again and a wave of fatigue sweeps over you. You struggle to throw off its effects.

Make a Fate Roll. If you wish to expend a point of Inner Force, you may add 2 to your Modifier for this roll only. If Fate smiles on you, turn to **80**. If Fate turns her back on you, turn to **92**.

57

Golspiel says that in that case it is his duty to inform you that his business affairs do not prosper under your rule and he is no longer able to afford to support the Watch. You will have to find an extra talent of gold from the treasury to pay them. You have thrown your lot in with Golspiel, and the shieldmaidens of Dama are unlikely to want to take over the manning of the Watch so you are stuck with the unpopular and harsh Antocidas and the mercenaries, who do little to increase your popularity. Note that you must now find a further talent of gold in tax and turn to **7**.

58

Sitting up, you grip the stone bridge firmly with your thighs and shunt your way forward. The Cyclops grins horribly and hefts another rock, sending it hurtling towards you. You must try to knock it aside with your iron-sleeved forearms. Treat this as a block, with a Defence of 8. If you knock it aside, turn to **310**. If not, turn to **118**.

59

That evening you attend evensong at the Temple to Kwon, prior to a private confessional with Parsifal. Parsifal leads the congregation at evensong just as he always has, but he does not say all the responses during the Catechism of the Redeemer, instead allowing one of the younger monks this privilege. After the service he walks alone into the Inner Sanctum, where you are to join him. It is a bare room which reminds you of the Temple of the Rock, covered with rush matting with the Song of Kwon inlaid in silver on the walls. Parsifal beckons you to kneel before him; his rheumy old eyes do not see as well as they did. 'Overlord?' he asks just to make sure it is you.

If you have the skill of ShinRen, turn to **389**. If not, read on. Will you kneel as normal (turn to **319**) or smash him to the matting using a Leaping Tiger kick (him to **329**)?

'What!' he exclaims. 'Why, I'll take you through the very Jaws of Forgetfulness themselves for that, sir,' and he smiles broadly, although you notice some of the crew making the warding sign against misfortune caused by the mention of the Jaws. You say, 'Yes, that would be fine, thank you.' He stares at you in amazement for a moment: 'Well, at least as far as the Haven of Tor,' he adds. You will have to find a boat of your own there. In truth you know you cannot expect simple fishermen to risk the Fangs, and you smile your agreement. A few hours later, you are scudding across a deep blue sea in perfect weather, a fair wind behind you and perilous adventure ahead. Your spirits soar and you send a prayer of joy and faith to Kwon.

Two days pass and you may restore another 3 points of lost Endurance. On the third day the Captain, who has ignored you up till now, says 'We shall arrive at the island tomorrow.' Will you ask him where you could find an Amulet of Nullaq (turn to **72**) or thank him and say nothing (turn to **414**)?

'So be it,' cries the Lord High Steward. 'Do not think that you can stand against the power of Nemesis, Lord of Cleansing Flame. Your reign will be short-lived. Your kingdom shall collapse around your ears, Avenger.' With that he stalks towards the exit. Will you order him to be thrown into the dungeons for his temerity (turn to **81**), fell him from behind with a throwing star (turn to **91**) or let him go free (turn to **101**)?

The swan-prowed boat glides forward at a word, angling closer to the right-hand rock. The water is a roiling maelstrom but the boat sails on. You grip its sides as it tries to hold its course through the heaving waters. The noise is deafening as the elvan boat bucks and shudders through the Fangs of Nadir. Suddenly the sea surges upwards as the rocks begin to close again. There is a sudden grating sound and the elvan boat shudders ominously. The right-hand wall of rock is not yet upon you but it seems a large section of rock juts out from it below the surface of the sea, for your boat is dashed amidships. It breaks up instantly and you are thrown into the sea. Desperately, you swim as fast as you can for the ever-closing gap, the heaving waters threatening to pull you under at any time. Suddenly you are in calmer waters, beyond the Fangs of Nadir. The rocks crash together behind you with a sound like thunder.

As you swim on you see a small island, not more than a half mile away. You guess it to be the one the Grandmaster of Shadows spoke of. You are a strong swimmer and the distance would be easy for you normally but between you and the island rages the Elemental Sea. It seems calm enough save where sudden geysers and spouts of water erupt randomly and whirl along at enormous speed for a little way, back and forth, raging around like a wall of water, before subsiding into the sea once more. The Sea is aptly named for these are Water Elementals. Taking a deep breath and sending a prayer to Kwon you dive into the water and strike out for the island.

Make a Fate Roll. If Fates smiles on you, turn to **54**. If Fate turns her back on you, turn to **74**.

63

Greystaff bows and says, 'I shall pray for you, Avenger,' before walking humbly from the Throne Room. Nobody around you seems particularly surprised or dismayed that you have not included Greystaff in the Council but there are those who hang their heads resignedly. Turn to **73**.

64

You twist and drive your foot up at your opponent's head. He reacts instantly, trying to cut at your leg as it flies up at him. If you succeed and you have the skill of Yubi-Jutsu, you may add 1 to the damage.

NINJA SENTINEL
Defence against Winged Horse kick: 8
Endurance: 13
Damage: *

If you win, turn to **148**. If you miss him, he jumps back and cuts at your extended leg, giving a short cry of triumph. The asterisk is to note your opponent need not roll for this attack or its damage; you lose 4 Endurance as he slices open your calf. If you still live, will you try a Dragon's Tail throw (turn to **52**), a Cobra Strike punch (turn to **76**), attempt another Winged Horse kick (return to the top of this paragraph) or will you try to relieve your opponent of his sword (turn to **160**)?

65

While the Master of the Chamber is attending you, one of the Palace servants enters the Banqueting Hall where you are breaking fast and says that a messenger from Golspiel waits outside with a message – for your ears only. Will you tell the servant to have the messenger escorted from the Palace, saying that Golspiel will stand trial for treason at noon (turn to **85**), ask the Master of the Chamber to wait outside and have the messenger admitted (turn to **358**), or keep the servant and Master by your side while the messenger shouts his message from the far end of the Banqueting Hall (turn to **105**)?

You jump up and launch a kick at one of the eunuchs' throats.

	1st BODYGUARD	2nd BODYGUARD
Defence against		
Leaping Tiger kick:	7	6
Endurance:	9	8
Damage:	1 Die + 2	1 Die + 2

If you have defeated them both, turn to **78**. If not, your Defence is 6 if both are alive, and you may block only one attack. If only one is left, your Defence is 8. If you survive, will you try a Dragon's Tail throw (turn to **114**), an Iron Fist punch (turn to **50**) or another Leaping Tiger kick (return to the top of this paragraph)?

The Demagogue is sporting a new purple tunic and breeches which make him look more like a badly-dressed court fop than the hero of the common people, but his ideas on taxation give the lie to this. To your surprise he begins his speech by saying that the expenses of the Crown should be no more than three talents and he would raise this money, and some to spare, in the following way: a window tax, that is a tax on all those people who owned buildings with more than ten windows in them, he has calculated would raise a talent of gold from the rich.

He also suggests a tax on all merchants with stalls or shops in the city, according to their size, which could raise a second talent. He then proposes a double tax on the Temple to Nemesis. In all, his measures would raise four talents and, 'it would endear you to the people, Your Majesty.'

Turn back to **7**.

As you step back, legs braced, arms poised to block, so does the figure in front of you. Suddenly you realise it is a mirror. From behind it, somebody utters a curse and the mirror is knocked forward to shatter at your feet. A man, pale and

gaunt, dressed in black robes adorned with whirlpool symbols, stands before you. It is a priest of Nemesis, chain-mace at his side.

'Only a fool would seek to enter this den of Scorpions and expect to live, Avenger, you mindless lackey of that weak-will so-called god of yours! May Nemesis, the Lord of Cleansing Flame devour your soul,' and he gestures with his hands, preparing a spell.

You leap forward, launching a Winged Horse kick, forcing him to jump back and abort his spell. He reaches for his mace as you attack again. Will you try a Tiger's Paw chop (turn to **104**), a Leaping Tiger kick (turn to **116**) or a Whirlpool throw (turn to **128**)?

69

Mandrake is a master of his trade. He struck too quickly for you. The swordstick which is now piercing your heart carries your name and the Rune of Everlasting Sleep upon it and you die. Mandrake escapes before the hue and cry is raised; no-one has ever survived his attention.

70

Your last blow took the Cyclops in the chest, sending it staggering backwards. It is unable to check itself and, with a great cry of fear, it topples into the chasm, its voice echoing away into nothingness. You will be unable to retrieve any shuriken you may have used.

You turn away and head up the path. It goes past a large cave mouth; a flicker of torchlight lights its interior. Will you enter the cave (turn to **95**) or continue up the path (turn to **286**)?

71

The doors from the vestibule open once more and the door-wardens bow as a tall, graceful woman clad in chain-mail strides purposefully into the Throne Room. Her short, spiky iron-grey hair and the calluses on her hands, caused by regular sword play, enhance her powerful presence. It is Force-Lady Gwyneth, High Priestess of the Temple to Dama,

Shieldmaiden of the Gods. If you have played Book 3: *USURPER!* but had no successful dealings with the Force-Lady, relying on the townspeople to rise up and throw off the cruel Usurper's yoke, turn to **221**. If instead the Force-Lady gave you a Statuette of the Goddess Dama as a token of her support for when the Usurper was overthrown, or if you did not read Book 3: *USURPER!*, turn to **211**.

72

His jaws open for a moment and he stutters in fear, 'On the Isle of Thieves – there is a Temple there to Nullaq, the Supreme Queen of Malice, whose touch is poison; many of her followers gain fortune and power... But you don't look like a reverencer of Nullaq – surely you know the ceremonies an initiate must go through! Surely you are not thinking of joining that vile, er, blessed cult!'

'No, I am not,' you say curtly. 'Thank you for the information.' He nods in relief, eyeing you oddly. However, he still backs away from you and avoids you for the rest of the trip.

An island looms ahead. A huge galley – a trireme with a single sail and triple rows of oars – comes past. Men dressed in bronze breastplates with greaves and crested helmets with cheek guards stand on deck, their round shields painted in many colours. 'A pirate ship from the island's fleet,' one of the fishermen mutters. However, it ignores your tiny fishing vessel. You decide to enter the port of the Isle of Thieves to try and steal an Amulet from the worshippers of Nullaq. Turn to **96**.

73

The sixth supplicant is a striking and impressive figure. It is Foxglove, head of the Usurper's secret informers, the Order of the Yellow Lotus, and a priestess of Nemesis. She is unusually beautiful and wears the rouge and eye paints of a courtesan while her look betokens a swift intelligence. She curtsies low before you, her wasp-waisted peacock-tail coloured dress a shimmering rainbow of greens and blues. 'Only the Lord High Steward knows as much as I of this city

and its people,' she says. 'The Steward is a symbol of the Usurper's tyranny. Oh yes, he tyrannised us too, Avenger; I counsel you to watch him carefully. But I can represent the many who revere Nemesis, winning them to your support, for though you have ended the time of our rule, life must go on for us too. A wise ruler will always have secret informers and I command a skilful Secret Society without whom you will never know a moment's security in this strife-torn city.' Her look as she finishes is one of challenge, as if she were almost daring you to accept her.

If you ask her to step into Star Chamber turn to **83**. If you disappoint her turn to **93**.

74

You are half way to the island when a great geyser of water erupts below you, lifting you into the air. Huge liquid arms seem to engulf you and, try as you might, you cannot escape their watery embrace. The Elementals plunge you to the depths and you drown far from home, in the Elemental Sea.

75

The Master of the Chamber announces that the first business before Star Chamber is the proclamation by the Overlord of his choice of a personal bodyguard. The monks of Kwon have, until now, been fulfilling this task, merely because they were on hand when you needed guarding. Alone as you are amongst the people of a city that contains many who are hostile to you, the choice of your personal bodyguard will be most important.

Will you choose to retain the services of your fellow monks, though their prowess at martial arts falls far short of those on the Island of Tranquil Dreams (turn to **175**) or will you draw a personal bodyguard from the ranks of the shieldmaidens (turn to **185**)? Or if Onikaba and his samurai came to your aid in Book 3: *USURPER!* you may wish to choose your bodyguard from these staunchly loyal élite troops. Turn to **195**.

Your enemy aims a vicious swipe at your head, but you anticipate the move and step inwards, taking his blade on your left forearm with a clang. You twist in to him and jab upwards at his throat. If you succeed and you have the skill of Yubi-Jutsu, you may add 1 to the damage.

NINJA SENTINEL
Defence against Cobra Strike punch: 8
Endurance: 13
Damage: 1 Die + 1

If you have beaten him, turn to **148**. If he still lives, he tries to gut you. Your Defence is 7 as you twist to avoid the wicked thrust. If you still live, will you try a Dragon's Tail throw (turn to **52**), a Winged Horse kick (turn to **64**), attempt another Cobra Strike punch (return to the top of this paragraph) or will you try to relieve your opponent of his sword (turn to **160**)?

Greystaff's look as he rises to address the Privy Council is both cold and determined. He draws himself up and then launches into a fierce harangue, listing the evils of the priests of Nemesis and the injustices heaped upon the Temples to Avatar and Kwon. He calls for a punitive tax of six talents to be levied against them and a further two talents of tax to be levied from the Temple to Time to be paid as reparations to his own temple and to the Temple to Kwon the Redeemer. 'Only thus can the wrongs of the Usurper be turned to right,' he says and is quite breathless and red in the face, through righteous anger, by the time he has finished. Turn back to **7**.

Bodies litter the ground around you. Hurriedly you take the Amulet from around the priestess's neck. The instant you touch it, your very soul is seared by a blast of ethereal energy. The pendant is utterly evil and you, as a bearer of an Amulet of Nullaq, have been tainted by its black sorcery.

Lose 1 point of Inner Force, permanently; you can never have more than 4 points of Inner Force until you find redemption. Mark this and the Amulet of Nullaq on your Character Sheet. You turn and leave, cursing your ill fortune. You feel unclean. You find lodging in an old stable for the night. You rise with the dawn and go down to the harbour. It is almost deserted but you notice a small untended single-sailed boat. Bold as brass you board it as if you owned it and cast off for the open seas. You leave the harbour unmolested and sail east towards the rising sun and the Fangs of Nadir. Turn to **38**.

79

The islands of the Inner Sea lie like emerald jewels in a flat plain of aquamarine. They are well populated; the people fish and trade olive oil, Murex shells from which purple dye is made, and strong red wine for other necessities. The sea is so clear that you can often see shoals of silver and red fishes trailing in the boat's wake until they are chased away by the porpoises which leap clear of the water for the sheer joy of living. Turn to **38**.

80

Using all of your willpower, you manage to shrug off the insidious effects of the priest's spell. He snarls in rage and jumps back, mace in hand, as you leap triumphantly to the attack. Will you use a Whirlpool throw (turn to **128**), a Leaping Tiger kick (turn to **116**) or a Tiger's Paw chop (turn to **104**)?

81

At your command two grey-robed monks bar the doorway. The Lord High Steward makes no fuss, merely allowing them to escort him to the dungeons in silence. The Throne Room is deathly quiet. You have imprisoned one of the most powerful people in the City of Irsmuncast without trial. This despotic act will be seen as a bad omen for times to come. Subtract 1 from your Popularity Rating, note that the Steward is imprisoned, and turn to **71**.

82

A gust of wind almost sends you plummeting off the bridge, and your heart leaps in your chest, but your superb sense of balance, honed to perfection after many years of training, keeps you in place. The Cyclops bellows and heaves a rock through the air at you. Make another Fate Roll as you try to duck below it, but subtract 1 from your Fate Modifier for this roll only, as there is so little room to manoeuvre. If Fate continues to bless you turn to **106**. If Fate deserts you turn to **118**.

83

Foxglove curtsies most elegantly once again and sweeps into Star Chamber. There is a discontented murmuring all around you for you have chosen the leader of that most despised section of Irsmuncast society, the infamous Order of the Yellow Lotus. Subtract 1 from your Popularity Rating. Note that Foxglove is one of your Privy Councillors on your Charter of Rulership. If you have now chosen four Councillors turn to **13**. Otherwise turn to **103**.

84

The dragon flaps its wings and descends to the ground, its head turned to the boy. You grab a spear dropped by a panicked militia man. Will you dash and try to drive the spear into the dragon's side (turn to **396**) or run forward, barge the boy aside and face the dragon yourself (turn to **144**)?

85

The messenger departs, unheard. If the Lord High Steward or Foxglove are Privy Councillors turn to **115**. If not, you dictate a statement regarding your dealings with Golspiel and the Werewolf to be read out in court. When the trial is concluded later in the day you are astonished to hear that the jury has acquitted Golspiel and set him free. If you act against him after his acquittal you run the risk of undermining your popularity so you decide to bide your time. You sweep, scowling, into Star Chamber. Turn to **145**.

86

The island looms ahead. A huge galley – a trireme with a single sail and triple rows of oars – comes past. Men dressed in bronze breastplates with greaves and crested helmets with cheekguards stand on deck, their round shields painted in many colours.

'A pirate ship from the Island's fleet,' one of the fishermen mutters. However, it ignores your tiny fishing vessel. You will have to enter the port of the Island of Thieves.

Turn to **96**.

87

The Privy Councillors wait in silence as you mull over the propositions that you have heard. Remember, you may not follow any advice that advocates the taxing of the Temple to Dama if you have already exempted that temple from tax.

Whose advice will you heed – that of Parsifal and Force-Lady Gwyneth (turn to **97**), or that of Greystaff (turn to **107**), Golspiel (turn to **117**), the Lord High Steward (turn to **127**), the Demagogue (turn to **137**) or Solstice (turn to **147**)?

88

You examine his posture and the way he holds himself, using the skills you learnt through the Training of the Heart. He is relaxed and seems to have no violent intent in his soul – at the moment. Confident he plans no deception, you move forward.

Turn to **100**.

89

You block the shieldmaiden's heavy blade, spin aside and floor her with a deft Winged Horse kick. A burning pain sears your back. It is not Parsifal who leapt to the attack, but Mandrake, Guildmaster of Assassins, from far-off Wargrave Abbas. He is a master of his trade. The blade which pierces your heart carries your name and the Rune of Everlasting Sleep. You die. No-one has ever survived the attention of Mandrake.

Fighting for balance in the boat, you send a shuriken spinning towards one of the huge unblinking eyes. It tears through the glutinous membrane, and a drop of greenish ichor wells up through the wound. The Kraken thrashes its tentacles in agony and you are sent flying through the air. You crash into the water, and when you come up you see the elvan boat intact, a few yards away from you. It is upside down, but, incredibly, it rights itself. You look around for the Kraken, but it is already sinking beneath the waves, returning to the watery depths to nurse its insignificant but painful wound. You swim to the boat and climb in and lie for a few moments, gasping for breath, after your ordeal.

The small island is close now and soon you are on the shore. The island is a round circle of earth only a hundred yards across. It is bare of vegetation and the air is cold and clammy, even though the sun beats down brightly from above. At the centre lies a cloud of mist, static and unmoving. You walk into it, and it billows about, chilling you to the bone. Then you emerge into a clearing, bounded by the mist, so that little light gets through.

A heap of skeletal remains lies piled to one side. Before it stands the Devil-Beast. It is humanoid, with great long arms that hang to the ground. Its hands are inordinately large, ending in vicious black talons. It half-squats, half-stands on two long legs – the thighs are peculiarly powerful, modified for jumping. The lifeless-looking skin is grey and warty, the head – vaguely elfin, but the nose – bulbous and misshapen. Great yellowed tusks protrude from its drooling mouth and its long thin hair is lank and matted with filth. Its eyes are dull, without intelligence, but they seem to blaze evilly with a malevolent red light. Elvan grace and beauty has been twisted into evil grotesqueness.

The Devil-Beast growls low in its throat, then nods at you. Blasts of scarlet energy lance from its eyes at you. If you have Acrobatics, turn to **302**. If not, your Defence is 6 as you try to dodge the unexpected attack. You cannot block this magical attack, either. If you are hit, turn to **264**. If not, turn to **276**.

91

In the twinkling of an eye you hurl a five-pointed throwing star at the unprotected head of the Lord High Steward. Make an Attack Roll.

If you score 9–12: Turn to **111**.
If you score 6–8: Turn to **121**.
If you score 2–5: Turn to **131**.

92

Try as you might, you cannot throw off the insidious effect of the priest's spell and you suddenly feel desperately tired. Your limbs are heavy, your reactions dulled. Subtract 2 from all your Modifiers for this fight only. If you manage to kill the priest, his spell will dissipate and you may restore your Modifiers to normal. The priest hefts his mace, grinning evilly. Desperately you launch an attack. Will you use a Whirlpool throw (turn to **128**), a Leaping Tiger kick (turn to **116**) or a Tiger's Paw chop (turn to **104**)?

93

Foxglove curtsies elegantly and sweeps out of the chamber, nose in the air. There is a sigh of relief from some of the Palace retainers. Turn to **103**.

94

A particularly strong gust of wind blows you off balance. You teeter horribly on the edge of the bridge. Not even your superhuman sense of balance, honed to perfection through years of training, can help you regain it and you fall off. Turn to **130**.

95

You enter the Cyclops's dwelling. It reeks with a foul stench of rotting flesh and excrement that hits your nostrils like a solid wall of odour. Retching, you look about. There is filth and rubbish everywhere. In one corner there is a heap of old clothes, weapons, splintered bones and so on – the remains of previous victims. Will you search through this heap (turn to **274**) or leave the cave and continue up the path (turn to **286**)?

96

The fishing sloop glides into the harbour of the Isle of Thieves. Scores of galleys – triremes and biremes – line the lengthy wood wharves. Bustle and activity surround you everywhere. Groups of ships, armed for piracy, arrow outward through the waves. A ship, heavy with booty and scarred by battle, limps inward. The wharves are lined with a milling crowd of sailors, cut-throats, villains and townsfolk – it is evident that the island's main trade is piracy. Your tiny boat is virtually ignored and you leap onto the quayside. Instantly, the fishing boat turns and leaves, without a by-your-leave, its Captain eager to be away from this place. You decide to explore the port, to see what you can learn. After a visit to a small clothing store, you enter the port itself looking, for all the world, like a typical one-eyed pirate on leave; at least the missing eye will be convincing enough, you think wryly to yourself.

You have been wandering about for a half hour or so when you cut through a narrow alley-way. You emerge to find yourself face to face with a large temple of ebon stone, its spider-like turrets and spires reaching heavenward in a seemingly random pattern. The enormous doors of lacquered red enamel are adorned with the symbol of a stylised spider, and priestesses dressed in red and black pass through it. Some of the buttresses are joined to the main building by arching spans of web, giving the impression that the whole place is but the abode of some great spider. You recognise a Temple to Nullaq, 'She who rules in malicious envy'. As you stare at it, wondering how mankind could fall to worshipping such evil gods and goddesses, a commotion behind you causes you to turn. It is a priestess of Nullaq, obviously of high rank for she has a bodyguard of two eunuchs, both naked to the waist. They are tall and heavily muscled, the muscle also covered with much fat. They wield enormous scimitars.

The little entourage emerges from the alley-way and

continues on their way, past the common folk, towards the temple. The priestess, in red and black, wears a strange head-dress of boiled leather, fashioned to look like the bloated body of a spider, a rather revolting sight. Your eye travels down the complicated array of robes to fix on that which hangs on a gold chain around her neck. It is a pendant of onyx, gilded with diamonds, shaped like a squid, an Amulet of Nullaq. It is too open for you to attack them now and they pass into the temple.

You need the Amulet. Will you hide on the rooftops of the alley in the hope another priestess will pass by, so you can ambush her (turn to 110), try to break into the temple to steal one (turn to 134) or wait until a ceremony is under way before breaking into the temple (turn to 122)?

97

The heads of the Temples to Kwon and Dama have proposed a crippling fine against the Temple to Nemesis, for the Usurper took most of the money for himself and squandered it or sent it across the planes to some dark treasure vault in the fires of the Abyss. The move is popular with the rest of your people, however, so increase your Popularity Rating by 1. If the Usurper's army is still in existence turn to 157. Otherwise you have completely bankrupted the Temple to Nemesis, received taxes as expected from the Temple to Time, and raised six talents for the treasury. If this is enough to meet the costs facing the Crown you have succeeded in raising enough taxes. If it is not enough you cannot afford to meet all of the Crown's debts and people mistrust you or think you are a weak Overlord. Subtract 1 from your Popularity Rating for each talent that you cannot afford to pay. If your Popularity Rating is now zero or below turn to 167. If it is above zero turn to 415.

98

You leap high into the air and somersault over the dragon's whipping tail. As you land on your feet, the dragon hisses in rage and shifts its body to face you. Then it opens its mouth and a bolt of electricity hurtles towards you. Your Defence is

6 as you try to avoid the bolt. If it hits you, turn to **198**. If it misses you, turn to **228**.

99

The mob is outraged and panics when you issue the edict which forbids Gwyneth to march out to battle. Your popularity slumps; the people's confidence in your rule is shaken badly as they wait helplessly for the Spawn of the Rift to lay siege to their city. Subtract 2 from your Popularity Rating.

If your Popularity Rating is now zero or less turn to **167**. Otherwise turn to **341**.

100

You stride slowly past him and his eyes follow you as you clamber up the rock-face. You can feel his gaze burning into your back, and a point between your shoulder blades begins to tingle. Resisting the temptation to look behind you, you climb on. It only takes a few minutes but it seems like an eternity to you – it is hard to believe this other ninja intends to let you pass freely. However, nothing happens and soon you are standing at the base of the three Crags of Abandoned Hope that tower above you.

The vista that stretches ahead takes your breath away. A valley opens up below, surrounded by mountain peaks. Unlike the barren and lifeless expanses of the Mountains of Undying Solitude, the valley is green and lush. You are looking down upon the fabled Valley of Scorpions, one of the most feared centres of evil on Orb, where the black-hearted ninja of Nemesis are trained. Outlying fields, extensively farmed, surround a small cluster of buildings in the middle of the valley. The village is enclosed by a man-high stone wall. You follow a winding goat track down.

Turn to **124**.

101

The Lord High Steward sweeps regally from the room and there is a general sigh of relief from the royal servants and other spectators. Turn to **71**.

102

Soon your little boat bears you into the harbour of Haven of Tor. It is a beautiful city – several tiers of white stone climbing skyward. Several galleys, triremes and biremes, are moored nearby. Some sails bear the symbol of a dancing sword, a tasselled scroll and an open hand beneath them – the symbol of Gauss the sage-god turned warrior-god. Others bear a pointed red cross on a white background, the symbol of the god Rocheval, lord of Paladins and Knights Errant. Warriors dressed in armoured breastplates, with greaves, round shields and crested helmets and bearing sixteen-foot pikes, patrol the harbour and man the city walls.

As you disembark at the bustling quayside you notice something odd about the city. Right across every inch of the city's rooftops and walls protrude vicious spikes, a good five feet in length. Each tier of the city walls is crested with many towers. Each turret contains several guardsmen, surveying the skies but not the outlying grounds. They man enormous ballistae, great crossbow-like devices pointed at the sky. Stretching between the towers are massive rope-nets, so that the whole city is encased in netting. You can only assume the city suffers from some terrible threat from the skies. You decide to investigate; if you can find nothing to aid you, at least you can wait till nightfall, when you can steal a more sea-worthy boat. Turn to **33**.

103

As soon as Foxglove's peacock-feather train has rustled out of the Throne Room, a tall and gaunt man in a grey and white robe with a broad white belt appears, as if from the air, before the throne. He bows slowly and then says, 'Greetings

Overlord.' It is Solstice, the High Priest of the Temple to Time. He says but one thing more: 'Time is on your side,' and awaits your decision. The noble face is lined with age but the wisdom that wells within the misty eyes is the wisdom of centuries. The priests of Time did not move a finger to help you against the Usurper, for all their legendary powers. You are forced to consider whether the support Solstice would bring is indispensable. Will you ask him to enter Star Chamber (turn to **361**) or disappoint him (turn to **123**)?

104

As the priest brings his mace down, you take it on your forearm and step in, delivering a punishing chop at his neck.

PRIEST OF NEMESIS
Defence against Tiger's Paw chop: 7
Endurance: 11
Damage: 1 Die + 1

If you win, turn to **140**. If he still lives, he swings the mace in a scything blow aimed at the side of your head. Your Defence is 7 as you try to duck beneath it. If you survive, will you try a Leaping Tiger kick (turn to **116**), a Whirlpool throw (turn to **128**) or another chop (return to the top of this paragraph)?

105

The rattle of armour presages the arrival of the messenger. He is a very tall man, about six and a half feet and seems almost as broad. His dark craggy face is disfigured by a purple scar running from his receding hairline to his ear and he sports a gold eye-patch. He wears scratched and supple cuir bouilli armour, the mark of his trade, and the servants have for some reason allowed him to bring his bastard sword into your presence.

'Since you will not vouchsafe me a private audience I cannot deliver my message, Your Majesty,' he says and bows low and quits the Banqueting Hall, leaving you to wonder what his message was.

If the Lord High Steward or Foxglove are members of the Privy Council of Star Chamber turn to **115**. Otherwise, you dictate a statement regarding your dealings with Golspiel and the Werewolf to be read out in court. When the trial is concluded later in the day, you are astonished to hear that the jury has acquitted Golspiel of the crime of High Treason and set him free. If you act against him after his acquittal you run the risk of undermining your popularity so you decide instead to bide your time, and sweep scowling into Star Chamber. Turn to **145**.

106

The rock flies over your head to shatter behind you, causing the bridge to shudder ominously. You reach the end and leap onto a wide ledge of rock, the Cyclops roaring in rage ahead of you. Behind it a path winds upward and out of sight around a weathered outcrop of stone. Turn to **142**.

107

You follow the advice of Greystaff, High Priest of the Temple to Avatar. Your action in fining the Temple to Nemesis and taxing heavily the Temple to Time splits the populace. The fine on the followers of Nemesis is crippling, for the Usurper took most of the money for himself and squandered it or sent it across the planes to some dark treasure vault in the fires of the Abyss. If the Usurper's army is still in existence turn to **157**. If not turn to **187**.

108

'What brings you to the Forest of Fables, Mortal?' Feeling that you can trust this Elf, you tell him who you are, of the City of Irsmuncast, and how you need the Orb and Sceptre to prevail against the forces of evil that threaten the lands of men in the north. You tell him of your need to pass the Fangs of Nadir, and, on impulse, you ask him for aid.

'The affairs of men are not really the concerns of elvankind, Avenger. Why should we aid you?'

Will you offer the Elf-Lord all the gold and gems in your possession (turn to **216**), say that a Devil-Beast guards the

Orb and Sceptre on the island and that you will slay it (turn to **234**), or say that Galanwiel and all his kin shall be forever welcome in the City of Irsmuncast if he aids you (turn to **306**)?

109

Solstice suddenly disappears, vanishing into thin air with a sound like a clap of thunder. The theatrics startle the courtiers, just as the High Priest's sudden appearance had in the first place. The door-wardens, however, keep their presence of mind and throw the doors wide open once more to admit Parsifal. His tired old body stoops slightly but the light of wisdom still burns in his eyes. You remember his fear when you announced that you had come to challenge the Usurper and his relief at your success. He does obeisance even though he is your senior in the temple hierarchy and says, 'I wish nothing more than to aid Your Majesty in re-establishing the rule of Kwon the Redeemer, through his intermediaries here on Orb.'

Will you invite him to take his place in Star Chamber (turn to **143**) or excuse yourself, saying that you will come to him for spiritual guidance but that you must win the support of another by granting the position of Councillor in his place? If you wish to do this you may send a royal messenger to recall one or more of the earlier supplicants (turn to **153**).

110

Clambering onto the rooftops on either side of the alley, you find a suitable place to lurk, behind a plaster chimney stack, at the back of a blacksmith's. Few people pass along this way until nightfall. You have been waiting motionless for many hours when another priestess of Nullaq, also with a guard of two eunuchs, comes down the alley. Luckily she bears the Amulet which is the symbol of her rank as well. They pass below you. If you have the skill of Poison Needles, you may jump down and spit one at the back of her neck (turn to **386**), or if you have the skill of Yubi-Jutsu, you can jump down behind her and drive a Tiger's Paw chop at the back of her neck (turn to **398**). If you have neither of these skills, or if you would rather not try the above options, you will have to jump down behind her and use your garrotte (turn to **408**).

111

The wickedly sharp throwing star has buried itself in the back of the Lord High Steward's head before anyone in the Throne Room realises what you have done. He hits the marble floor with a crack, stone dead. Two servants drag his body away and another gives you the Purple Jade Ring which he wore; note it on your Character Sheet. There is grim silence as you await the next supplicant. You have certainly cowed your new subjects, but your despotic act, killing one of the most powerful citizens out of hand, is seen as an augury of bad things to come under your rule. Subtract 1 from your Popularity Rating and turn to **71**.

112

You walk forward slowly and then suddenly lash out with your foot in a Winged Horse kick. You catch him by surprise but his reflexes are honed to perfection and he manages to slap your foot aside with his hand. He leaps back, a prodigious bound, and shouts, 'You are not of the Scorpion! Prepare to die.' With that he reaches over his back and draws the short sword with dazzling speed. You circle each other warily. The other ninja holds his sword at his side, then gives a guttural cry and darts forward onto one knee and slashes at your legs. You leap nimbly over the flashing blade and launch an attack of your own. Will you try to slide under his guard and execute a Dragon's Tail throw (turn to **52**), try a Winged Horse kick (turn to **64**) or try to close in and drive a Cobra Strike up at his throat (turn to **76**)?

113

Your vision blurs. Solstice seems to disappear and then reappear before you. Wordless, the High Priest of the Temple to Time walks slowly towards the Council Room as if troubled by a wasting disease. Note that he is one of your four Privy Councillors on your Charter of Rulership. If you have now chosen all four, turn to **13**. Otherwise, turn to **133**.

114

You slide at one of the guards in an attempt to sweep his feet from under him. You may choose which one to attack.

	1st BODYGUARD	2nd BODYGUARD
Defence against		
Dragon's Tail throw:	5	6
Endurance:	9	8
Damage:	1 Die + 2	1 Die + 2

If you are successful, he topples over and you sit up driving a Tiger's Paw chop at his neck. His Defence is 6 and you may add 2 to your Punch Modifier and damage for this attack.

If both are dead, turn to **78**.

If either one survives, they slash at you with their serrated scimitars. If two are alive, your Defence is 6 and you may block only one attack. If only one is left, your Defence is 8. If you still live, you may try an Iron Fist punch (turn to **50**) or a Leaping Tiger kick (turn to **66**).

The representatives of the faction which reveres Nemesis have formulated a plan. If the Lord High Steward is not otherwise indisposed, he joins Foxglove in outlining a strategy. To begin with, Foxglove – who today wears a scarlet and black gown which leaves her shoulders bare – warns you that unless steps are taken to ensure otherwise, the jury will have been bribed before the trial and Golspiel will be acquitted. She suggests that you use the Order of the Yellow Lotus to keep watch over the jurors.

If available, the Lord High Steward, still dressed in black and silver, solemn as ever, adds that if handled properly Golspiel's trial could be the end of your money problems: 'Golspiel is the richest man in the city, by far, most of it ill-gotten gains. Strip him of his possessions and the treasury will be full to overflowing. You will be able to rule with a free hand. Without this money there will be a great many problems facing you.' Clearly Golspiel is popular with nobody.

Will you respond graciously to the advice and act on it (turn to **155**) or reject the plan, saying that justice must find its true course (turn to **165**)?

You hop forward and leap up, driving the ball of your foot at his head with deadly force.

PRIEST OF NEMESIS
Defence against Leaping Tiger kick: 8
Endurance: 11
Damage: 1 Die + 1

If you win, turn to **140**. If he remains standing, he swings the mace up at your stomach. Your Defence is 6 as you try to jump backwards. If you survive, will you try a Whirlpool throw (turn to **128**), a Tiger's Paw chop (turn to **104**) or another Leaping Tiger kick (return to the top of this paragraph)?

117

When it comes to money matters Golspiel of the Silver Tongue is a genius. Your tax system is seen to be fair and effective although many wish you had fined the Temple to Nemesis more heavily. From the sale of Indulgences and temple taxes the treasury receives seven talents of gold. If this is enough to meet the cost facing the Crown you have succeeded in raising enough taxes. If it is not enough you cannot afford to meet all of the Crown's debts and people mistrust you or think you are a weak Overlord. Subtract 1 from your Popularity Rating for each talent that you cannot afford to pay. If your Popularity Rating is zero or below turn to **167**. If it is above zero turn to **415**.

118

The rock, about the size of your chest, crashes into your shoulder with numbing pain. Lose 3 Endurance. The impact bowls you off the bridge. Turn to **130**.

119

Fed up with being cooped up in the Palace, out of touch with the common people, you decide to don the disguise of a journeyman and walk the streets. Fear hangs over everybody like a black pall. The city wall on the Edgeside has been all but breached and men toil to repair the damage before the next onslaught. You are watching the labour when a small child walks up to you and greets you by name in a dreamy far-away voice: 'Listen to your dreams, Avenger; the way will be shown.' The message given, she shakes her head and the glazed look leaves her eyes. Seeing you, a complete stranger as she thinks, she shrieks and flees.

You go to sleep that night pondering over your strange meeting. The voice of Kwon the Redeemer enters your dreams bringing guidance at last: 'Since the glorious days of Telmain I, the rulers of Irsmuncast have wielded two powerful artefacts – the Sceptre and Orb. Without them, Avenger, your rulership is doomed. These artefacts were reft from your father and carried away to the Mountains of Undying Solitude, within which lies the Valley of Scorpions where the evil ninja of the Way of the Scorpion live and train. You must there defeat their Grandmaster of Shadows, for it is he who knows the whereabouts of the Sceptre and Orb.'

You awake next morning with new resolve. You shall seek these artefacts.

The subsequent proclamation is heard all over the city. Overlord Avenger I is to bring back the Luck of Irsmuncast, the Orb and Sceptre of Telmain. The heroic nature of your quest to the Mountains of Undying Solitude appeals to the people who seem to forget that you are deserting them in their darkest hour. It is not too late to change your mind. Will you do as bidden by your god (turn to **409**) or stand beside your people in their hour of need (turn to **315**)?

120

As fast as you can you spit a needle at one of the huge glutinous eyes. It sinks in and disappears from view but the Kraken does not even notice – the needle is a speck of dust to it and the poison has no effect at all. It tilts the boat and drops you into its mouth, boat as well, and its snapping beak slices you in two. Death is instantaneous.

121

The throwing star buries itself in the Lord High Steward's shoulder before anyone in the Throne Room realises what you have done. The Lord High Steward spins round to face you, then spins twice more, quickly. His cloak billows around him like a silver and black whirlpool, the symbol of Nemesis, and then a pillar of silver fire erupts above him like a swirling silver waterfall. The Lord High Steward has cast the spell of the Cleansing Fire. The silver fire swirls towards you. Will you dive behind a nearby group of royal servants (turn to **141**), somersault over the fire if you have the skill of Acrobatics (turn to **151**), try to disbelieve the fire – it may be an illusion (turn to **161**), or order the Lord High Steward to dispel his magic fire of death (turn to **171**)?

122

It is that very night that many lay worshippers of Nullaq – ordinary citizens of this port of thieves – begin to enter the temple. If you have the skill of Climbing, you may scale a rooftop and try to climb one of the temple's turrets, whilst the temple guards and priestesses are involved in whatever ceremony is about to be performed (turn to **156**). If you do not have Climbing skills, or do not want to scale the tower, you can join the milling throng of worshippers (turn to **278**).

123

Solstice nods slowly and then says in a voice heavy with boredom, 'The reign of your father the Loremaster – the reign of the Usurper after him – these were but as the blinking of an eye to me and so it shall be with your reign. It matters not; the final outcome will be no different.' With that he is gone amid noise like a clap of thunder. Turn to **411**.

124

Soon you can make out small figures moving amongst the fields and buildings and you decide to leave the path, striking out across the valley-side, so as to approach the village from a less obvious quarter. There is nothing below to suggest that ninja inhabit the village, but you feel sure that all those rough-looking farmers and mountain villagers are adepts of the Way of the Scorpion in disguise. Nor do any of the buildings look large enough to be suitable as training halls and there is certainly nothing to suggest that this is the only other Ryu, or school, outside the Island of Plenty for the Way of the Scorpion on Orb. Will you descend to the village straightaway (turn to **196**) or wait in hiding until nightfall (turn to **208**)?

You accept the offer of ten talents of gold and set Golspiel free. Sure enough, mule-loads of gold arrive at the Palace before sundown. The treasury has never been so full but the word spreads like wildfire that Golspiel has bought you off just as he has others before you. Your popularity slips as you are seen to be little better than a corrupt official who accepts a bribe. Subtract 1 from your Popularity score.

Turn to **145**.

The spear-head clatters harmlessly off its iron-like scales. The dragon snaps its head forward and gobbles up the boy in one fell swoop. There is a cry of anguished rage behind you. Paladin is on his feet and he charges at the dragon howling in a frenzy. The white sword slices through the dragon's scales like a knife through butter – black ichor bubbles forth. The dragon rears back in pain, and Paladin leaps forward, plunging the blade into its pulsing belly. The dragon bellows in agony and tries to escape, but Paladin, enraged, proceeds to hack it to pieces. Never have you heard tell of so large a dragon so easily bested by one man. When it is over the red and black dragons break off their attack in dismay. Paladin absent-mindedly thanks you for trying to help, but then turns and walks away, head bowed, deep in grief.

There is nothing more for you here, so you decide to leave. You hurry down to the harbour-side where you find a suitable boat easily – nobody is about. It has a single sail and looks sturdy and reliable. Soon the city recedes from sight as you head out to open sea. Turn to **79**.

When the rumour circulates that you have set your taxes along the lines proposed by the Usurper's Lord High Steward there is a public outcry. The people are angry that you have not punished the priests of Nemesis with a heavier tax. Subtract 1 from your Popularity Rating. You now have five talents of gold in the treasury. If this is enough to meet the cost facing the Crown you have succeeded in raising enough taxes. If it is not enough you cannot afford to meet all of the Crown's debts and people mistrust you or think you are a weak Overlord. Subtract 1 from your Popularity Rating for each talent that you cannot afford to pay. If your Popularity Rating is zero or below turn to **167**. If it is above zero turn to **415**.

128

As the priest swings his mace at your head, you step in and grab his wrist. Your other hand reaches for his robes, ready to twist him over your hip. But the priest says a word, unintelligible to your ears, untrained as you are in the ways of magic. Suddenly a shock of energy leaves the priest's arm and crackles through your body, jerking you backwards and causing you to lose 2 Endurance.

If you still live, the priest laughs and closes in again. You recover quickly and attack again. Will you try a Leaping Tiger kick (turn to **116**) or a Tiger's Paw chop (turn to **104**)?

129

The monk grimaces in agony as your iron sleeve cracks his shin and he sails over your head as you duck, then collapses in a heap behind you. You step quickly towards Parsifal who, surprisingly, has already regained his feet. He whips a swordstick out from under his robe, revealing a surprisingly muscular chest as he does so. As you halt in shock a fount of acid spurts from its tip as if by magic, blinding you. This is not Parsifal, you realise too late, but Mandrake, Guildmaster of Assassins, from far off Wargrave Abbas, who worships Torremalku the Slayer, swift-sure bringer of death to beggar and king.

In unseeing desperation you whirl your arms in a blocking motion but Mandrake knows his trade. The swordstick carries your name upon it and the Rune of Everlasting Sleep. One skilled thrust and it pierces your heart, ending your life. Mandrake kills your bodyguards and is away before the hue and cry is raised. No one has ever survived his attention.

You plummet through the air; the world seems to spin around you as you tumble down. You hit the net and lie there breathless, bobbing up and down above the floor of the chasm hidden in shadows far, far below you. The Cyclops laughs triumphantly. It leans down over the side of the chasm and grabs some ropes that hold the net. Sitting on the bridge, it shunts to the other side and grabs the other edge of the net. Then it returns once more to the side from where it appeared and reels in the ropes, chuckling all the while.

The net comes loose and you start in fear for a moment as it falls downwards, but the Cyclops takes your weight easily. As you hang there, the creature twists and spins you, until you are totally enmeshed in the net, before it hauls you up and stomps off up the path, dragging you behind it. A dark cave mouth looms ahead and the Cyclops drags you in and tosses you in a corner. The cave smells of rotting meat and there is a foul stench of excrement. By this time you are hopelessly caught up in the net, unable to move your limbs. The Cyclops starts to pile wood onto an old fireplace of piled stones, muttering phrases like, 'Roast man-thing,' and smacking its lips. Old bones gnawed and splintered testify to its grisly eating habits. Amidst these remains lies a mound of clothing, weapons and so on heaped in a corner, the possessions of other victims. If you have the skill of Escapology, turn to **154**. If not, turn to **166**.

The wickedly sharp throwing star buries itself in the lintel just above the Lord High Steward's head, but he doesn't so much as break stride as he sweeps majestically towards the doorway. If you wait in silence for the next supplicant turn to **71**. If you order him to be clapped in irons in the dungeon turn to **81**.

The Elf-Lord looks closely at you and then says, 'Why, you are an Elf-Friend. Welcome indeed, my friend. How is it you came to friendship with the elvan-kind?' You tell him the story of Lithuel. When you have finished he is grim-faced: 'One day we shall be avenged upon the vile church of Nullaq.' Then he smiles at you and says, 'I am at your service, sir. Ask and we shall do our best to aid you.' You tell him of your quest and he looks thoughtfully at you as you speak. 'To pass the Fangs of Nadir into the Elemental Sea is a perilous dash,' he says, 'but we can aid you in this. Follow us.'

You follow them into the forest until you come to an area where the trees are less dense but much taller. Each tree is the home of an elvan family, living on tiered tree houses. You are led to the bank of a rushing river where several boats are moored. They are of white wood, with beautifully carved swan prows.

'These are enchanted elvan boats, Mortal, and they respond to spoken commands. All you need do is tell the boat the direction you wish to travel in, and it shall bear you there. With one of these you should be able to survive even the Fangs of Nadir.'

The Elf-Lord wishes you well, saying that this, the river Greenfen, runs to the Inner Sea. 'Head north, and then east to reach the Fangs.' You climb into one of the boats and an Elf casts you off. You command the boat forward and it sails sedately away. Turn to **252**.

133

Solstice suddenly disappears, vanishing into thin air with a sound like a clap of thunder. Quivering with expectancy, you wait for those haunting old eyes to reappear but start in surprise when instead the door-wardens who, it seems, have only seen Solstice appear once, throw the doors wide open once more to admit Parsifal. His tired old body stoops slightly but the light of wisdom still burns in his eyes. You remember his fear when you announced that you had come to challenge the Usurper and his relief at your success. He does obeisance even though he is your senior in the temple hierarchy and says, 'I wish nothing more than to aid Your Majesty in re-establishing the rule of Kwon the Redeemer, through his intermediaries here on Orb.'

Will you invite him to take his place in Star Chamber

(turn to **143**) or excuse yourself, saying that you will come to him for spiritual guidance but that you must win the support of another by granting the position of Councillor in his place? If you wish to do this you may send a royal messenger to recall one or more of the earlier supplicants (turn to **153**).

134

You circle the temple, examining it for the best way to enter. In a little-frequented sidestreet at the rear of the temple lies a servant's entrance – for food, tradesmen and so on. Night falls and the port is plunged into darkness. But it seems to become even more lively than in the day and the streets are thronged with revellers, hawkers, villains and thieves. Will you try to gain entrance at the side door (turn to **146**), or if you have the skill of Climbing, scale the rooftops and then onto the temple spires (turn to **156**)?

135

Antocidas reacts almost as though you had slapped him. Without Golspiel he will probably lose his position as leader of the mercenaries. He plainly cannot believe that you can walk away from such wealth. When he recollects himself, a dark scowl crosses his face and he turns on his heel and walks out. You have made another enemy.

If the Lord High Steward or Foxglove are members of the Privy Council of Star Chamber turn to **115**. Otherwise, you dictate a statement regarding your dealings with Golspiel and the Werewolf to be read out in court. When the trial is concluded later in the day you are astonished to hear that the jury has acquitted Golspiel of the crime of High Treason and set him free. If you act against him after his acquittal you run the risk of undermining your popularity so you decide instead to bide your time, and sweep scowling into Star Chamber. Turn to **145**.

136

There is no answer. If you have the skill of Arrow Cutting, turn to **28**. If you have not, turn to **40**.

In following the advice of the Demagogue you have captured the public imagination as a fair and just ruler. You tax the rich to give to the poor or so the word goes in the taverns and cockpits. Add 1 to your Popularity Rating. By not taxing the temples you are making the lives of the people cosier for they are not called on to make donations at their temples. You have only raised four talents for the treasury, however. If this is enough to meet the cost facing the Crown you have succeeded in raising enough taxes. If it is not enough you cannot afford to meet all of the Crown's debts and people mistrust you or think you are a weak Overlord. Subtract 1 from your Popularity Rating for each talent that you cannot afford to pay. If your Popularity Rating is zero or below turn to **167**. If it is above zero turn to **415**.

You rear back in terror, but the Kraken, a daughter of Nullaq, seems to respond to the magical, and evil, aura of the Amulet. Its tentacles cease to writhe and the hideous monstrosity sinks down, quiescent. Slowly it disappears, back into the watery depths. The small island is close now and soon you are on the shore. The island is a round circle of earth only a hundred yards across. It is bare of vegetation and the air is cold and clammy, even though the sun beats down brightly from above. At the centre lies a cloud of mist, static and unmoving. You walk into it, and it billows about, chilling you to the bone. Then you emerge into a clearing, bounded by the mist, so that little light gets through.

A heap of skeletal remains lies piled to one side. Before it stands a Devil-Beast. It is humanoid, with great long arms that hang to the ground. Its hands are inordinately large, ending in vicious black talons. It half-squats, half-stands on two long legs – the thighs are peculiarly modified for jumping. The lifeless looking skin is grey and warty, the head – vaguely elfin, but the nose – bulbous and misshapen. Great yellowed tusks protrude from its drooling mouth and its long thin hair is lank and matted with filth. Its eyes are dull, without intelligence, though they seem to blaze evilly

with a malevolent red light. Elvan grace and beauty has been twisted into evil grotesqueness.

The Devil-Beast growls low in its throat and then nods at you. Blasts of scarlet energy lance from its eyes at you. If you have Acrobatics, turn to **302**. If not, your Defence is 6 as you try to dodge the unexpected attack. You cannot block this magical attack, either. If you are hit, turn to **264**. If you avoid it, turn to **276**.

139

You order Foxglove to do nothing. You will act just as you would normally. Parsifal leads his congregation at evensong just as he always has, but he does not say all of the responses during the Catechism of the Redeemer, instead allowing one of the younger monks this privilege. After the service he walks alone into the Inner Sanctum where you are to join him. It is a bare room which reminds you of the Temple of the Rock, with rush matting and with the Song of Kwon inlaid in silver on the walls. Parsifal beckons for you to kneel before him; his rheumy old eyes do not see as well as they did. 'Overlord?' he asks just to make sure it is you.

If you have the skill of ShinRen, turn to **389**. If not, read on. Will you kneel as normal (turn to **319**) or smash him to the matting using the Leaping Tiger kick (turn to **329**)?

140

The priest falls backwards, dead. You step over the body and press on. After a few yards the corridor opens out into a circular well, a spiral staircase going down. You look over the edge – a bright light glows at its base, a hundred yards below. The whole effect is that of a whirlpool and you realise the staircase was built in honour of Nemesis, the god whose symbol is the vortex.

Alert for any sign of traps, you descend the stairs. You come out in a well-lit, spacious chamber. The floor is of polished wood and the walls polished ebony, lined with glowing lanterns. It is bare of furniture, save an altar at the other end, with a black velvet drape, covered in striking white whirlpool and scorpion shapes, lain over it. An idol towers behind it, a powerfully built hawk-headed man, naked but for a plain black kilt. The arms are raised and the eyes stare ahead. It radiates an aura of evil and you recognise the figure as an effigy of Nemesis.

Before the altar a man sits cross-legged. He is dressed in the costume of a ninja, but red in colour and without the hood. A black cloth belt is tied around his waist. His forearms are exposed. A scorpion is tattooed on each wrist. His face is nondescript, instantly forgettable, save for the eyes, black as night and full of power and malice. On the floor in front of him rests an unusual weapon, a kyoketsu-shoze. A length of braided animal hair connects a heavy metal ring to a dagger-like blade.

'Welcome, Avenger,' he says, his voice blank and unaccented, so that it could not be recognised again. 'I did not expect you to get this far. You have done well. But now you have come to the end. I am the Grandmaster of Shadows, Master of the Way of the Scorpion, supreme form of ninjutsu. No mere adept I, but the most accomplished ninja on Orb.'

He rises to his feet, the kyoketsu-shoze in his hands. You stand facing each other, about fifteen feet apart, each daring the other. Then the Grandmaster whirls the dagger and ring about his head in a complicated series of movements. He utters a short cry and sends the iron ring hurling towards your head. Will you try to catch the ring (turn to **152**) or try to dodge it (turn to **164**)?

As the spiral of flame pirouettes closer, you dive from the throne and roll behind a group of your servants who are dumbstruck by the apparition. The approaching whirlpool of fire erupts with a bang as soon as it touches them, burning a young page boy and an aged retainer to death. The Lord High Steward has swept regally from the room before you regain your feet. A deathly hush falls in the room as the bodies are removed and you await the next supplicant in silence. The courtiers and servants are not impressed by your cowardly behaviour; it appears that the Lord High Steward has got the better of you. Subtract 2 from your Popularity Rating and turn to **71**.

142

The Cyclops balls its hammer-like fist and, head down, charges at you, bellowing loudly. You avoid its bulk with ease and then move in to attack. Will you use a Forked Lightning kick (turn to **322**), an Iron Fist punch (turn to **334**) or the Dragon's Tail throw (turn to **346**)?

143

Parsifal steps into Star Chamber and the Throne Room is silent once more. Note that the High Grandmaster of the Temple to Kwon is a Privy Councillor on your Charter of Rulership. If you have now chosen all your Councillors it is time to join them in Star Chamber (turn to **163**). If not you will have to send a royal messenger after one or more of the earlier supplicants (turn to **153**).

144

You dash forward and hurl yourself at the boy. He is knocked aside and you turn to face the dragon, spear at the ready. The huge head fills your vision, the great jaws lined with massive teeth; two eyes malevolent and bright with intelligence look down on you mockingly. It opens its mouth and unleashes a bolt of electric energy that streaks towards you. Your Defence is 6 as you try to avoid it. If it strikes you, turn to **198**. If it misses you, turn to **228**.

145

There is a pregnant silence in the council chamber as, obviously displeased, you enthrone yourself. You will have to be careful of assassination attempts while men as wealthy and powerful as Golspiel and as dangerous as Antocidas the One-Eyed are at large. The Master of the Chamber announces that the first business before Star Chamber is the proclamation by the Overlord of his choice of a personal bodyguard. The monks of Kwon have, until now, been fulfilling this task, merely because they were on hand when you needed guarding. Alone as you are, amongst the people of a city that contains many who are hostile to you, the choice of your personal bodyguard will be most important. Will you choose to retain the services of your fellow monks, though their prowess at martial arts falls far short of those on the Island of Tranquil Dreams (turn to **175**) or will you draw a personal bodyguard from the ranks of the shieldmaidens (turn to **185**) – or if Onikaba and his samurai came to your aid in Book 3: *USURPER!* will you choose your bodyguard from these staunchly loyal élite troops (turn to **195**)?

146

You casually approach the door and walk in. A woman sits in a chair, one hand on a lever, some ten feet away from you down a thin corridor; there is a door behind her. 'You did not give the signal,' she says as she pushes the lever. The floor opens below you and you fall helplessly down a hole. You plummet into a large carven chamber. The floor is covered in a thousand sharpened steel spikes, clustered together – skeletons and rotting bodies still impaled upon them. You can do nothing as you fall upon the spikes, and you are killed instantly.

147

As Solstice suggests, you do not tax the Temple to Time. You are accused of favouritism but this move does not seem to have actually affected your popularity. The tax on the other temples brings five talents into the treasury. If this is enough to meet the cost facing the Crown you have succeeded in raising enough taxes. If it is not enough you cannot afford to meet all of the Crown's debts and people mistrust you or think you are a weak Overlord. Subtract 1 from your Popularity Rating for each talent that you cannot afford to pay. If your Popularity Rating is zero or below turn to **167**. If it is above zero turn to **415**.

148

The ninja aims a final cut at your head but you hop forward and lash out with a Leaping Tiger kick, smashing the incoming wrist, breaking it. He grunts in pain and his weapon flies away. As your leg hits the ground you jump up and whip your other foot into the ninja's temple, killing him instantly. You step over the inert body and begin climbing the rock-face. Soon you are standing at the base of the three Crags of Abandoned Hope that tower above you.

The vista that stretches ahead takes your breath away. A valley opens up below, surrounded by mountain peaks. Unlike the barren and lifeless expanses of the Mountains of Undying Solitude, the valley is green and lush. You are looking down upon the fabled Valley of Scorpions, one of the most feared centres of evil on Orb, where the black-hearted ninja of Nemesis are trained. Outlying fields, extensively farmed, surround a small cluster of buildings in the middle of the valley. The village is enclosed by a man-high stone wall. You follow a winding goat track down. Turn to **124**.

149

Your bodyguards slam the doors shut behind you and there is the sound of a scuffle within Star Chamber. If the Lord High Steward is one of your Privy Councillors turn to **169**. If not, turn to **179**.

150

You are about to leap when one of its tentacles crushes the Elves' boat like matchwood. Suddenly there is nothing to leap from and you drop straight into its gaping maw. Its snapping beak slices you in two. Death is instantaneous.

151

As the spiral of flame pirouettes closer, you spring from the throne into a piked somersault, drawing a gasp of amazement from the courtiers as you sail towards the ceiling and then land nimbly. The approaching whirlpool of flame erupts with a bang as it hits the throne but no-one is harmed. The Lord High Steward turns to leave. Will you order him to be clapped in irons in the dungeon (turn to **181**) or merely wait in silence for the next supplicant (turns to **71**)?

152

With deft accuracy your hand closes around the ring, inches from your face. Suddenly, the Grandmaster whips the animal hair and twists it around your wrist with a practised flick of his arm. He *wanted* you to catch it! You are caught off balance and he yanks you towards him, the dagger in his other hand. As you stumble up to him, he thrusts at your mid-section. You twist but the blade slides across your ribs. Lose 4 Endurance. If you still live, you dive forward and past the Grandmaster, somersaulting to your feet, ripping your wrist out of the braided hair. As you spin to face him, he hurls the dagger at you, the corded hair streaking after it. Will you try to catch the dagger and attempt to yank it away from him as soon as you have it (turn to **176**) or try to dodge it (turn to **188**)?

153

You may invite any of the earlier supplicants to join you in Star Chamber unless, that is, you have imprisoned or killed them. If Foxglove is among those you choose, turn to **173**. Otherwise, when you have completed your choice, it is time to join your Councillors in Star Chamber (turn to **163**).

154

You wriggle and twist, dislocating your joints until you are able to release your left arm. The Cyclops, its attention on the fire, does not notice you. Using a shuriken you saw away at the rope until you have cut your way free. As silent as a ghost you stand, the Cyclops' broad back some six feet ahead

of you. Will you use your garrotte (turn to **178**), use Poison
Needles, if you have that skill (turn to **190**), step forward
and drive an Iron Fist punch at the back of its neck, using
Inner Force (turn to **202**) or drive an Iron Fist punch at its
neck, but without Inner Force (turn to **214**)?

155

If the Lord High Steward was brought up from the dungeon,
where he had been clapped in irons, to speak before you,
then you may set him free now if you wish. If not, he is
returned to the dungeon.

If he is alive and free, he joins Foxglove in organising
things so that Golspiel is indeed found guilty. Foxglove also
proves conclusively that he had bribed some of the jury and
she has them charged. Golspiel is exiled from Irsmuncast,
never to return on pain of death, and his wealth is seized by
the Crown. At one stroke you have filled the treasury, for he
was indeed one of the richest men alive. Choice baubles from
his mansion house are chosen to decorate your bed-
chamber; a stuffed manticore, the jewels of Pandar, and the
Tulemite vases are amongst the haul. As the riches flow into
the Palace the next council session begins. Turn to **75**.

156

You ascend a warehouse roof with ease. Opposite you an
ebon tower rises high. Fastening on your cat's claws to feet
and hands, you swing the grappling hook out. It fastens to a
hideous gargoyle high above. After testing the anchorage,
you fasten the rope to your waist and swing out, to hang
below the tower's top. Slowly and silently you crawl up the
spire, like a fly, using your cat's claws and the rope.

Eventually, you are sitting on the head of the gargoyle,
high above the port of the Isle of Thieves. The streets are
alive with activity and the sounds of a lawless city are wafted
to you on a night breeze, laden with the stink of the dregs of
humanity. You climb on up, until you come to an open
window at the top of a single turret. A shaft of moonlight
reveals a web of thin strands woven across the inside. You
know each strand, if touched, will set off an alarm. But you

have dealt with such traps before. You roll into a handstand so that your vision is low to the ground, enabling you to pick out the strands strung across the floor, and you carefully walk on your hands across the room, avoiding contact with every gossamer-thin thread. It is painstakingly slow but at length you reach the door opposite. You listen at the door, but all is quiet. Do you have the skill of Picking Locks, Detecting and Disarming Traps? If so, turn to **170**. If not, turn to **182**.

157

Incensed at the financial burden you have placed upon them the priests of Nemesis lead the Usurper's army against you in counter-revolution. If your Popularity Rating is 5 or above turn to **197**. If not, the people do not lift a finger to help you. The Palace is surrounded and broken into, your bodyguards slain and, after a fierce struggle, you are taken and broken on the wheel in sight of the Temple to Kwon the Redeemer. Evil rules in the city once again.

158

'A noble quest, Avenger. But to pass the Fangs of Nadir! Perilous indeed. However, I can help you there. On the coast to the south of the Fangs is the Forest of Fables. It is inhabited by Wood Elves and their lord is Galanwiel. He and I are old friends. Here, take this ring,' and he gives you a Gold Signet Ring bearing a carven lion upon it — note it on your Character Sheet. 'I will give you a boat, and you can sail there — it is but a few days' travel. The Elves will find you in the forest. Give this ring to Galanwiel and say to him I sent you. He will aid you.'

You thank Paladin and he orders a boat to be prepared for you. Soon you are at sea in a small but sturdy sail boat, heading east, away from the setting sun. Two days later a shoreline looms up ahead and you pull the little boat up onto the sandy beach. A thick wall of trees stretches away to either side where the beach ends. You walk towards them and enter the forest.

Turn to **26**.

159

There is a spluttering and fizzing sound underneath the oval table and the room suddenly begins to fill with smoke. Parsifal staggers jerkily towards you as if fighting against a spell. 'Kill him, Avenger!' shouts Foxglove. Will you pull Parsifal to safety outside the room (turn to **229**) or bury a throwing star in his face (turn to **309**)?

160

The battle rages on, each of you seeking a weakness in the other's defence. You lure your opponent into thrusting his sword at your belly and you sidestep the blade, trying to clamp it to your side with your arm, a manoeuvre requiring perfect precision and co-ordination. Treat this as if you were making an attack, but you do not have any plus or minus Modifiers. Your enemy's Defence is 6. If you succeed, turn to **184**. If you fail, turn to **172**.

161

The improbable spiral of silver flame pirouettes closer and erupts with a loud bang when it touches you. It was no illusion. Your ninja costume falls from you in piles of ashes; the pain is almost unbearable and you sink to your knees, forced to call upon your Inner Force to avoid blacking out. Subtract 1 from your Inner Force, unless you have the skill of ShinRen, in which case you triumph over your pain.

The Lord High Steward has departed before you regain your senses; nobody dared to stop him. You have been bested by the Usurper's Steward in your own Throne Room and he has escaped. You are horribly wounded but the scars will heal in time. The people doubt your strength as a ruler; subtract 2 from your Popularity Rating. A new costume is brought and your wounds salved while you await the next supplicant in brooding silence. Turn to **71**.

162

During the next tenday, reports begin to come in concerning an ominous build-up of troops at the edge of the Rift. It seems that an army of sorcerous Dark Elves and terrible

Cave Trolls is preparing to attack Irsmuncast. If Force-Lady Gwyneth heads the Watch and is a Privy Councillor, *and* leads the shieldmaidens of Dama in your army, turn to **201**. If Gwyneth does not hold *all* of these positions of power turn to **341**.

163

Is Force-Lady Gwyneth, High Priestess of the Temple to Dama, a member of the Privy Council? If she is, turn to **203**. If she is not, turn to **213**.

164

At the last instant you react and spin away to face him once more. He whips the ring back to him and sends the dagger hurtling towards you, the braided hair streaking behind it. Will you try to catch the dagger and attempt to yank it away from him, (turn to **176**) or simply try to dodge it (turn to **188**)?

165

Foxglove quits the room with a look of utter disdain – the Lord High Steward, if present, remains impassive. The session with the council is postponed until the verdict of Golspiel's trial is brought to you, for which you dictate a statement regarding your dealings with Golspiel and the Werewolf to be read out in court. When the trial is concluded later in the day you are astonished to hear that the jury has acquitted Golspiel of the crime of High Treason and set him free. If you act against him after his acquittal you run the risk of undermining your popularity so you decide instead to bide your time, and sweep scowling into Star Chamber. Turn to **145**.

166

Try as you might, you cannot move. The huge Cyclops, once its fire is lit, takes a huge wooden club and comes over to you. 'Bye-bye man-thing,' it grates and chuckles loudly. You are unable to avoid the club and it crashes down on your head, dashing out your brains. Death is instantaneous.

167

Public support for your rule is at a low ebb and the priests of Nemesis choose this time to whip up feeling against you. The dark tide of counter-revolution sweeps the city and no-one lifts a finger to help you. The Palace is surrounded and broken into, your bodyguards slain and, after a fierce struggle, you are taken and broken on the wheel in sight of the Temple to Kwon the Redeemer. Evil rules in the city once again.

168

The heavy tail cracks across your legs as you try to leap over it. Lose 4 Endurance. The dragon turns on you as you get to your feet and opens its mouth. A lancing bolt of electricity hurtles towards you. Your Defence is 6 as you try to avoid the bolt. If it hits you, turn to **198**. If it misses you, turn to **228**.

169

The sounds of scuffling end abruptly and then the Lord High Steward's voice rings out, 'Overlord, you may safely return. We have dealt with the imposter.' Will you go back in (turn to **209**), or follow the advice of your bodyguards and return to your study (turn to **179**)?

170

Your one good eye picks out a slight hairline crack in the door jamb. Investigating it, you find that a small panel comes away to reveal a mechanism that will propel a poisoned needle into the doorway if it is opened. Deftly you disarm it and step through. Then you freeze, every sense alert. You stand stock-still and look down. Your foot rests upon a thin wire stretched across the doorway. It is taut, pinned under your foot. Straight ahead of you a panel in the opposite wall has opened, revealing a small crossbow bolt, ready to launch itself at your chest. You know that the slightest movement of your foot will set it off. You have no choice but to dive to the right into the corridor ahead and try to avoid the bolt. Without hesitating, you hurl yourself forward in a somersault.

Make a Fate Roll. If Fate smiles on you, turn to **230**. If Fate turns her back on you, turn to **254**.

171

The Lord High Steward hesitates; your imperious tone of command has momentarily shaken his confidence. The spiral of silver flame shivers and dies as he turns to leave. Will you order the Lord High Steward to be clapped in irons in the dungeon, (turn to **181**) or choose to calmly await the next supplicant (turn to **71**)?

172

As fast as you are, the Scorpion Ninja divines your purpose and he twists the blade so that the cutting edge forces into your side. Desperately you abort your manoeuvre and the ninja whips his sword back trying to slice open your rib-cage as he does so. Your Defence is 6 and his attack will do 1 Die + 1 damage. If you still live, will you attempt a Dragon's Tail throw (turn to **52**), a Cobra Strike punch (turn to **76**) or a Winged Horse kick (turn to **64**)?

173

When you order the messenger to carry the news to Foxglove there is a discontented murmuring all around. You have chosen the leader of the most despised section of Irsmuncast society, the infamous Order of the Yellow Lotus. Subtract 1 from your Popularity Rating and turn to **163**.

174

You show Galanwiel the ring and tell him your tale and ask for his help.

'As it is Paladin's wish, we shall give help to you,' he replies. 'To pass the Fangs of Nadir into the Elemental Sea is a perilous task but we can aid you in this. Follow me.'

You follow him deep into the forest until you come to an area where the trees are less dense but much taller. Each tree is the home of an elvan family, living on tiered tree houses. You are led to the bank of a rushing river where several boats are moored. They are of white wood, with beautifully carved swan prows.

'These are enchanted elvan boats, Mortal, and they respond to spoken commands. All you need do is tell the boat the direction you wish to travel in, and it shall bear you there. With one of these you should be able to survive even the Fangs of Nadir.'

The Elf-Lord wishes you well, saying that this, the river Greenfen, runs to the Inner Sea. 'Head north, and then east to reach the Fangs,' he finishes. You climb into one of the boats and an Elf casts you off. You command the boat forward and it sails sedately away. Turn to **252**.

175

Your announcement that the monks of Kwon will be your personal bodyguards causes no surprise. Henceforth, there will be two monks close to your person at all times and these will be reinforced with more whenever you leave the Palace. Note your bodyguard and turn to **205**.

176

Roll for a block. Your Defence is 6 as you attempt to catch the dagger. If you are successful, turn to **200**. If you fail, turn to **212**.

'My men are ready to serve you, Avenger. I am a wealthy man who knows the vagaries of this city. It is well known that the treasury's coffers are empty; I can fill them for you. I am wise in the ways of the world and so it is my pleasure to offer myself up to you as adviser. You will find that the problems which beset your rule will be many – more than you can imagine. I have lived through the hard times of the tyrant's rule and know how to turn things to profit. Money, influence, good counsel, friends in other cities – all of these I offer. Will you take them?' He smiles, his eyes almost hidden in the creases of his cheeks. He is undoubtedly a wily fellow who seems to have made a second fortune while the Usurper was sucking the city dry. Will you invite him to step into Star Chamber (turn to **351**) or disappoint him (turn to **288**)?

You glide forward and whip the wire around the beast's massive neck, driving your knee into its gargantuan back. The Cyclops gurgles disgustingly, a thin red line appearing like magic around the corded muscles of its neck. It growls and surges to its feet, lifting you into the air. Eyes bulging, it reaches backwards and grasps you with its massive arms. Its strength is terrible and it pulls you over its head and throws you at the wall of the cave, bellowing in rage. If you have the skill of Acrobatics, turn to **226**. If not, turn to **238**.

The doors to Star Chamber burst open suddenly and Parsifal appears, his robes in disarray to show part of a surprisingly muscular chest. Foxglove lies still on her back under the oval table within. Before you realise what is happening he produces what looks like a swordstick which glistens wetly from within his grey habit and attacks you with the skill of a champion swordsman. This is no old man, certainly not Parsifal; with a flash of recognition you realise that this is Mandrake, Guildmaster of Assassins from far away Wargrave Abbas. Honoric and others have offered him half

a king's ransom to kill you, and Mandrake has never been known to fail. You decide to attack as the dripping point of the swordstick thrusts at your chest. Will you dodge aside and use the Whirlpool throw (turn to **189**) or try the Forked Lightning kick (him to **199**)?

180

You have misjudged the blow, and all you have accomplished is to leap right into its gaping jaws. Instantly they snap shut, crushing you, and you are swallowed up – a light snack for the dragon.

181

At your command two grey-robed monks bar the doorway. The Lord High Steward makes no fuss, merely allowing the monks to escort him to the dungeon in silence. You have got the better of the Usurper's Lord High Steward after he tried to defeat you using the hideous spell of the Cleansing Fire. It was the act of a despot to imprison him without trial but it will be seen as an omen that you are a strong ruler. Add 1 to your Popularity Rating, note that the Steward is imprisoned, and turn to **71**.

182

You push the door open gingerly. There is a muted click and a thin needle jabs out from the door jamb, puncturing your arm, and then retracts again. The wound is negligible, but it begins to burn ominously. The needle was tipped with poison. If you have Immunity to Poisons, turn to **218**. If you do not have this skill, turn to **206**.

183

As per his habit, Solstice does not deign to stand to address the Council. He wraps his grey and white robes close about him before beginning: 'The Temple to Time is like an island in this city, between the factions of good and evil, law and chaos. We ask for nothing and, traditionally, we give nothing, save of course for advice which we hope will prove useful. It is thus appropriate that the Temple to Time should continue to be exempt from tax. As to the others I suggest a one-talent tax for the Temples to Dama, Kwon and Avatar, two talents for the priests of Nemesis who fared well under the Usurper's rule. This I feel would help to return affairs in the city to a balanced state whilst also raising five talents in tax. I am sure Your Majesty appreciates the support of our priesthood and does not want to dispense with it.' The old priest catches your eye and holds it, as if divining your thoughts. Turn back to **7**.

184

With incredible dexterity you are able to dodge the sword and trap it under your left arm, causing your opponent to gasp in astonishment. Your right hand grips the top of the blade near the hilt and you tug. However, instead of resisting you, the other ninja merely flicks his wrist. There is a click and the hilt of his sword comes away, another small dagger-like blade protruding from it, leaving you with the full length of the sword. The momentum of your attempt to pull it free causes you to stagger back and your opponent darts, spins and slashes at your face with the dagger. Your Defence is 7 against this attack and his dagger will do 1 Die damage if it connects. If you still live, you drop the now useless sword-blade. You may attack your opponent once more, but you may not try to disarm him again. However, note that the ninja's Defence is reduced by 1 as he cannot keep you at bay with his sword, his Attack Roll is also reduced by 1, and his damage becomes 1 Die unless otherwise specified. Will you attempt a Dragon's Tail throw (turn to **52**), a Cobra Strike punch (turn to **76**) or a Winged Horse kick (turn to **64**)?

185

Your announcement that the shieldmaidens of Dama will be your personal bodyguard raises a few eyebrows but nothing is said. Henceforth there will be two shieldmaidens close to your person at all times and these will be reinforced whenever you leave the Palace. Note your bodyguard and turn to **205**.

186

The Kraken reaches out for the boat and a tentacle coils around the prow, and begins to lift it. Will you stay in the boat (turn to **210**), or leap out and take your chances in the sea (turn to **242**)?

187

The Temple to Nemesis claims they are beyond their means when they have paid four talents of gold and so this is all you can raise from them. Their priests are incensed and seek any excuse to retaliate. The priests of the Temple to Time, led by Solstice their High Priest, refuse to pay the two-talent tax. The city did not react as favourably as you hoped to your tax policy and you may lack the support to force them to pay. If you wish to attempt this, under the hostile eye of the Temple to Nemesis, turn to **197**.

If not, you have four talents in the treasury. If this is enough to meet the costs of the Crown you have succeeded in raising enough taxes. If it is not enough you cannot afford to meet all of the Crown's debts and people mistrust you or think you are a weak Overlord. Subtract 1 from your Popularity Rating for each talent that you cannot afford to pay.

If your Popularity Rating is zero or below turn to **167**. If it is above zero turn to **415**.

188

You duck below the flying dagger and he yanks it back, catching it deftly in his hand. He nods his head wryly and you realise that he wanted you to catch it. Then he shouts and leaps high into the air to land before you, the dagger in one hand, the iron ring twirling about his head in the other. He is close enough for you to attack as he stands there smiling, mocking you.

Will you try to wipe the smile off his face by jumping up and lashing your instep round at the right side of his head (turn to **224**) or wait for him to make a move (turn to **236**)?

189

You have dodged just in time. A fount of acid pours forth like a geyser from the tip of the swordstick, as if by magic. It would have blinded you but instead you step forward and grab Mandrake's sword-arm before whirling him round and dashing his head on the floor. Before he can recover, you deliver a crushing blow to the side of his neck which kills him outright. Your bodyguards have hardly had time to move but now they whisk you away to your private quarters, as the Councillors, including Foxglove who looks very dazed, leave Star Chamber. Even though you have been relying more on your wits than your body of late, your reactions appear not to have suffered. Mandrake's disguise was perfect; without Foxglove's help you might well be dead. You send a message of thanks and tomorrow there will be a banquet to celebrate your survival. Turn to **419**.

190

Placing a needle on your tongue, you edge forward and blow hard. It flies forward and embeds itself in a meaty shoulder blade. The Cyclops grunts in pain, and then surges to its feet and turns on you. It roars in rage and picks up a massive wooden club which it twirls menacingly. Then its face goes grey and it staggers drunkenly. But it does not go down, much to your surprise; its massive body seems able to withstand the venom. It is, however, momentarily disorientated. You decide that to try and throw so large a target would be pointless. Will you use a Leaping Tiger kick (turn to **250**) or an Iron Fist punch (turn to **262**)? You may add 2 to your Modifier for your first attempt only, as it is briefly disorientated.

191

The crossbow bolt grazes your thigh and you feel the burning heat of poison. This time it is too much for your body's immunity system and you cannot fight off the waves of nausea and pain. Burning in agony, you slump to the floor, twisting uncontrollably. You die in great pain.

You leap high into the air and somersault over the dragon's whipping tail. As you land on your feet, the dragon hisses in rage and shifts its body to face you. Then it opens its mouth and a bolt of electricity hurtles towards you. Your Defence is 6 as you try to avoid the bolt. If it hits you, turn to **198**. If it misses you, turn to **228**.

The merchant bows before beginning his speech, in which he outlines *his* idea of the amount of money the treasury needs and then suggests ways of obtaining it. Firstly, he suggests that the five main temples – to Kwon, Dama, Time, Avatar and Nemesis – be taxed at the rate of one talent each. In addition, he proposes the sale of Indulgences, a system whereby the Overlord bestows baronetcies and other honorary titles on people who are willing to pay for that honour and the favour of the Crown. He estimates that this will bring in a further two talents, meaning that you would collect seven talents overall. His arguments are persuasive and he points out that these measures should not prove unpopular, while raising a great deal of money.

Turn back to **7**.

An island comes into view and a port reveals itself when you round a rocky headland.

'Haven of Tor' says the Captain happily, 'where our ways part, and we can head for home.'

Haven of Tor is a beautiful city, several tiers of white stone climbing skyward. Several galleys – triremes and biremes – are moored nearby. Some sails bear a symbol of a dancing sword, a tasselled scroll and an open hand beneath them – the symbol of Gauss the sage-god turned warrior-god. Others bear the pointed red cross on a white background, the symbol of the god Rocheval, Lord of Paladin and Knights Errant. Warriors dressed in armoured breastplates with greaves, round shields and crested helmets, and bearing sixteen-foot pikes, patrol the harbour and man the city walls.

As you disembark at the bustling quayside you notice something odd about the city. Right across every inch of the city's rooftops and walls, protrude vicious spikes, a good five feet in length. Each tier of the city walls is crested with many towers. Each turret contains several guardsmen, surveying the skies, not the outlying grounds. They man enormous ballistae, great crossbow-like devices pointed at the sky. Stretching between the towers are massive rope nets, so that the whole city is encased in netting. You can only assume the city suffers from some terrible threat from the skies. You decide to investigate. If you can find nothing to aid you, at least you can wait till nightfall, when you can steal a sea-worthy boat. Turn to **33**.

195

Your announcement that Onikaba's samurai will be your personal bodyguard causes consternation even though they are peerlessly loyal and superb warriors. Henceforth there will always be two samurai close to your person at all times and these will be reinforced whenever you leave the Palace. These men are incorruptible and tirelessly alert. Unfortunately, the people of Irsmuncast resent your choice of foreigners as your personal bodyguard. Reduce your Popularity Rating by 1, note your bodyguard, and turn to **205**.

196

It is not long before you have reached the valley floor. You move like a shadow through the fields, towards the village. You think you have not been spotted when you reach the village's edge but suddenly a score of figures, ninja like you, emerge as if from nowhere, and are joined by several more from turfed-over pits in the ground. You are surrounded. One of them says, 'Welcome to the Valley of Scorpions, lackey of Kwon.' You fight valiantly, taking several with you, but there are simply too many of them and you are cut to ribbons in minutes.

Fighting breaks out in the streets once more, but you have enough support to defeat the forces of the Temple to Nemesis and what was previously the Usurper's army for a second time, but only after a fierce struggle, during which a fire started by children burns down a part of the city. Your popularity is going down. Subtract 2 from your Popularity Rating. You have managed to squeeze four talents out of the Temple to Nemesis which is transferred to the treasury. If this is enough to meet the costs of the Crown you have succeeded in raising enough taxes. If it is not enough, you cannot afford to meet all of the Crown's debts and people mistrust you or think you are a weak Overlord. Subtract 1 from your Popularity Rating for each talent that you cannot afford to pay. If your Popularity Rating is now zero or below turn to **167**. If it is above zero turn to **415**.

You duck down but the bolt skims your shoulder, before striking the courtyard, where it shatters a slab of marble. The bolt has seared you — lose 3 Endurance. It rears its head back preparing to snap at you with its great jaws. As it comes down, will you now drive a Leaping Tiger kick right at the tip of its nose, using Inner Force (turn to **348**), try to drive your spear into its gaping maw (turn to **294**) or hurl two shuriken as fast as you can into its mouth (turn to **330**)?

As your foot lashes out to knock the swordstick aside, a fount of acid pours forth like a geyser from the tip of the swordstick as if by magic. You never deliver the real attack for the acid has blinded you. In unseeing desperation you whirl your arms in a blocking motion but Mandrake knows his trade. The swordstick carries your name upon it and the Rune of Everlasting Sleep. One skilled thrust and it pierces your heart, ending your life. Mandrake kills your bodyguards and is away before the hue and cry is raised. No one has ever survived his attention.

200

Deftly you catch the shortened dagger hilt, a feat of extraordinary skill. The Grandmaster is surprised for a brief moment and you tug at it with all your strength, ripping the kyoketsu-shoze out of his hands. The ring lands, clattering at your feet. Immediately, your enemy somersaults backwards into a hand-stand and continues to flip backwards to the altar. He reaches it and takes up a scabbarded ninja sword from behind it. As you disentangle the cord from your arm and cast it aside – it would be useless in your untrained hands – he jumps towards you again, coming to a halt some four feet in front of you. His left hand is on the scabbard, his other on the hilt, poised to draw. If you have the skill of ShinRen, turn to **272**. If not, turn to **296**.

201

You have put much faith in Force-Lady Gwyneth and this is certainly not misplaced, but the people of the city now idolise her. She is seen to be as powerful as you are yourself and she is more popular as well. When the rumour of attack by the Spawn of the Rift ignites the city, the streets become thronged with people crying aloud to the Force-Lady to deliver them from danger. The priests of Nemesis, quick to exploit the mob's hysteria, call upon her formally to lead the army out to battle. The mood of the mob brooks no hesitation. If you wish to order Gwyneth to march towards the Rift in the hope of victory, turn to **355**. If you refuse to bow to mob hysteria and order her to defend the walls of the city, turn to **99**.

202

You glide up behind the massive back, pausing briefly to call up your reserves of inner strength, then drive your fist at its neck, uttering a cry as the Inner Force leaves you. The blow, laden with power, cracks its skull like an egg and it slumps forward, dead. It never even uttered a sound. Will you search the heap of bric-a-brac in the corner (turn to **274**) or leave the cave and head on up the pathway (turn to **286**)?

Before you can join your Privy Councillors in the chamber, a royal messenger arrives with news that there is tension in the streets due to there being no law-keeping force or Watch at present. You stride into Star Chamber intent on solving this problem first. Star Chamber is a large oval room, the ceiling of which is black marble covered with five-pointed stars in gold leaf. A large marble table separates a small throne on one side from four tall straight-backed chairs in which your chosen Privy Councillors sit. Standing near your throne is a clerk in emerald green robes, the Master of the Chamber. You beckon him and, in an undertone, tell him of the unrest in the streets. He asks you if you wish to make this the first item on the agenda and you agree. He convenes your first session of Star Chamber and tells your Councillors that the first issue is that of immediate civil unrest. He then invites the four Councillors to give advice. Turn to **373**.

There is nothing you can do against this huge monstrosity; as a tentacle as thick as you are closes around your waist, your ribs crack and it draws you beneath the waves. You cannot break its hold and you are drowned before it swallows you up in one bite.

The next item on the agenda is the fate of the army. In the fighting most of the forces, particularly the Orcs, remained loyal to the Usurper, only changing sides when all seemed lost. Perhaps two hundred were slaughtered, including General Barkant, but they still number nigh on four thousand sword-arms: about a thousand Orcs, the same again of the noseless crossbreed Halvorcs, plus two thousand humans – almost all men. The great bulk of them are loyal to Nemesis, but loyal also to their city. The problem facing you is one of dilemma. On the one hand, they help to protect the city against raids from the Bowels of Orb so without them the city's military defence strength will be weakened. On the other, certain of their captains long to revenge the humiliation of their defeat when the Usurper was overthrown, so if you allow any of them to remain in your new army they will be a constant threat to you.

If any of the following are present – the Demagogue, Force-Lady Gwyneth, the Lord High Steward, Greystaff or Solstice – they place their clenched fists on the table, indicating that they wish to speak. Anyone present who does not do so either has no advice to give or does not *wish* to give any. You may call upon any or all of your four Privy Councillors to speak in the following order:

The Demagogue: Turn to **215**.
Force-Lady Gwyneth: Turn to **225**.
The Lord High Steward: Turn to **235**.
Greystaff: Turn to **245**.
Solstice: Turn to **255**.

If you have heard everyone, or all you want to hear, turn to **265**.

206

The venom races through you and you sink, twitching, to your knees, your body on fire. Too late you remember the words of the Book of the Gods, 'Ware poison in the Temple to Nullaq.' It reaches your heart and you are dead within seconds.

207

On the day after the hunt banquet, Star Chamber is due to meet again. A young boy brings a message while you are being dressed, from Foxglove, head of the Order of the Yellow Lotus, the secret informers. It consists of two words, written in puffs of rouge on the back of a silver hairbrush – 'Ware Parsifal'. Puzzled as to why you should be wary of the High Grandmaster of the temple to your own god you ask the servant to fetch Foxglove, but there is no time to speak to her before the session in Star Chamber begins. The Master of the Chamber, wearing scarlet and green today, announces that the first item on the agenda is the fate of the Order of the Yellow Lotus, the secret informers, led by Foxglove. If present, the Privy Councillors mentioned below indicate that they wish to speak. You may ask them to speak in this order:

The Lord High Steward: Turn to **227**.
Parsifal or Force-Lady Gwyneth: Turn to **237**.
Foxglove: Turn to **247**.
Greystaff or the Demagogue: Turn to **257**.

When you have heard all you can or wish to hear, turn to **267**.

208

A rocky enclave provides a suitable hiding place and you rest for the remainder of the day, meditating and observing the village below. The thought that you are amongst the most deadly and most evil assassins on Orb fills you with worry at times. As evening falls you notice that several 'villagers' climb down the well at the centre of a cobbled square, rather than go to any of the houses. No doubt the real centre of the ninja base lies below ground. When night has fallen over the valley, like a cloak, you move down into the fields. Everything is quiet save for the muted scratchings of crickets and the occasional hoot of an owl. The valley would be idyllic if it weren't for its inhabitants. You pass through the night like a shade, flitting from tree to bush, unseen in the moonlight. As you near the stone wall, some kind of sixth sense tells you all is not as it should be. If you have the skill of Picking Locks, Detecting and Disarming Traps, turn to **418**. If not turn to **220**.

209

You push open the doors to Star Chamber once again to find Foxglove and the Lord High Steward flanking a figure who looks like Parsifal but who is pointing a swordstick at you. The priest and priestess of Nemesis speak identical Words of Power and you feel as if you are being sucked down into a whirling black vortex. Nausea overcomes you and you stumble forward. A fount of acid pours forth like a geyser from the tip of the swordstick, blinding you. As you stagger helplessly, Mandrake, Guildmaster of Assassins from far-off Wargrave Abbas, buries the tip of the swordstick in your heart. He knows his trade well. The blade is engraved with the name 'Avenger' and with a Rune of Everlasting Sleep. He will collect his blood money for your death, thanks to the treachery of Foxglove and the Lord High Steward.

210

It lifts the boat clear out of the water and it is all you can do to stay in it. You are on a level with its enormous lidless eyes, its bulbous body – a sickly putrid cream colour – below you. The great maw opens wide, ready to devour you.

Will you try to hurl a shuriken at one of its eyes (turn to **90**), use Poison Needles, if you have that skill, to spit a needle at one of its eyes (turn to **120**) or try to leap out of the boat into the sea (turn to **150**)?

211

It was Force-Lady Gwyneth and her shieldmaidens who began the successful revolution against the Usurper in return for your promise to restore the laws and customs of your father, the Loremaster. These included appointing the shieldmaidens of Dama to patrol the city and keep the Watch. Gwyneth bends on one knee before the throne; then plants her feet firmly apart and says in her low firm voice, 'My thanks for delivering our city from the tyrant, Your Majesty. I know that you, a worshipper of Kwon the Redeemer, appreciate that without the just rule of law this city will lose its sinews and its strength until, at last, it will be overwhelmed by the evils of the Rift or our foes in the western Manmarch. As a symbol of law and a just leader, I would be a loyal adviser in Star Chamber. May I remind you that General Barkant was killed in the fighting yesterday. The army is without a leader. I have already ordered the Usurper's troops to be confined to barracks and my own troops are even now on the streets, controlling the looting.'

She looks you calmly in the eye, awaiting your decision. Will you invite her to step into Star Chamber (turn to **231**) or disappoint her (turn to **241**)?

You have misjudged the speed of the dagger and your hand closes on empty air. The blade sinks into your shoulder. Lose 4 Endurance. If you still live, the Grandmaster yanks it back, causing you to gasp in pain; he catches the returning dagger deftly in one hand. Then he shouts and leaps high into the air to land before you, the dagger in one hand, twirling the iron ring about his head in the other. He is close enough for you to attack as he stands there smiling, mocking you. Will you try to wipe the smile off his face by jumping up and lashing your instep round at the right side of his head (turn to **224**) or wait for him to make a move (turn to **236**)?

Before you can join the Councillors, a breathless royal messenger strides into the Throne Room and kneels before you. 'There is widespread looting and pillaging, Your Majesty. A fire has started in Pudding Lane and there will be others if we cannot restore order. The whole city may burn. The poor are terrorising the rich and the priests of Nemesis are threatening reprisals.' You thank the messenger and stride into Star Chamber to take advice on this matter.

Star Chamber is a large oval room, the ceiling of which is black marble decorated with five-pointed stars in gold leaf. A large marble table separates a small throne on one side from four tall straight-backed chairs in which your chosen Privy Councillors sit. Standing near your throne is a clerk in emerald green robes, the Master of the Chamber. You beckon him and, in an undertone, tell him of the unrest in the streets. He asks if you would like to make that the first item on the agenda and you agree. He convenes your first session of Star Chamber and informs your Councillors that the first issue is that of immediate civil unrest. He then invites the Councillors to give their advice. Turn to **233**.

You glide up behind the beast and drive your fist with all your power at its neck. There is a meaty crash and it falls forwards writhing in agony and bellowing loudly. However, it still lives, and it lumbers away from you, snatching up a huge wooden club as it does so. You will have to fight it, but note that it has lost 6 from its Endurance of 19. You decide that to attempt a throw on so large a target would be pointless. Will you now use a Leaping Tiger kick (turn to **250**) or an Iron Fist punch (turn to **262**)?

215

The Demagogue rises to his feet and spreads his arms theatrically: 'What need have we of a professional army? Are we followers of Moraine, god of Empire, wishing to subdue all the lands of men under our dominion? Our walls are tall and strong. There are twenty thousand able-bodied men and women in the city needing no more than elementary instruction in the arts of war to become a fine fighting force, buoyed up with revolutionary ardour. Why not form a citizens' volunteer militia and do away with the exorbitant cost of the army at a stroke? The people can defend their city from the spawn of the Rift.' Turn back to **205**.

216

His face falls. 'What need have we for gold and gems? You think to buy the services of the Elves,' he says, outraged. 'You are not a creature of evil, and we will let you pass freely through our forest, but we will not aid you.' With that the Elves melt away into the greenery.

Shrugging your shoulders, you press on through the forest. A day and a night pass uneventfully – it is as if the forest inhabitants are avoiding you, even though you move with the stealth of a panther. You rest well in any case, and you may restore 3 points of lost Endurance.

At last you emerge from the forest to stand on the shores of the Elemental Sea. A small island lies not more than half a mile out to sea; you guess this to be the one the Grandmaster of Shadows spoke of. You are a strong swimmer and the distance would be easy for you normally but between you and the island rages the Elemental Sea. It seems calm enough save where sudden geysers and great spouts of water erupt randomly and whirl along at enormous speed for a little way, back and forth, raging around like a wall of water, before subsiding into the sea once more. The sea is aptly named, for these are Water Elementals. Taking a deep breath and sending a prayer to Kwon, you dive into the water and strike out for the island.

Make a Fate Roll. If Fate smiles on you, turn to **54**. If Fate turns her back on you, turn to **74**.

217

On the day after the hunt banquet Star Chamber is due to meet again. A young boy brings a message while you are being dressed from Foxglove, head of the Order of the Yellow Lotus, the secret informers. It consists of two words, written in puffs of rouge on the back of a silver hairbrush, 'Ware Parsifal'. Puzzled as to why you should be wary of the High Grandmaster at the temple to your own god you ask the servant to fetch Foxglove, but there is not time to speak to her before the session in Star Chamber begins. The Master of the Chamber, wearing scarlet and green today, announces that the first item on the agenda is the fate of the Order of the Yellow Lotus, the secret informers, led by Foxglove. If present, the Privy Councillors mentioned below indicate that they wish to speak. You can ask them to speak out in this order:

Gwyneth: Turn to **317**.
Foxglove: Turn to **327**.
Greystaff or the Demagogue: Turn to **337**.
The Lord High Steward: Turn to **347**.

When you have heard all you can or wish to hear, turn to **357**.

218

The deadly venom courses through your blood; you sink to your knees, waves of nausea and pain flowing over you. But your years of training and your resistance to poison enables you to withstand its effects. After a few minutes you stand on shaking legs, groggy and dizzy. When you have recovered you push the door open and step through. Then you freeze, every sense alert. You stand stock-still and look down. Your foot rests upon a thin wire stretched across the doorway. It is taut, pinned under your foot. Straight ahead of you, a panel in the opposite wall has opened, revealing a small crossbow bolt, ready to launch itself at your chest. You know that the slightest movement of your foot will set it off. You have no choice but to dive to the right into the corridor ahead and try to avoid the bolt. Without hesitating, you hurl yourself forward in a somersault.

Make a Fate Roll. If Fate smiles on you, turn to **230**. If Fate turns her back on you, turn to **191**.

219

The two samurai rush forward between you and Parsifal as he pulls a swordstick from the folds of his robe, revealing, as he does so, a surprisingly muscular chest. Even as he flourishes the wetly dripping swordstick, a fount of acid pours forth from its tip as if by magic, blinding both of the samurai. Were it not for their swift and loyal action it would have been you who was blinded. From deep within your memory you dredge up the identity of your assailant. This is not Parsifal but an impostor – Mandrake, the Guildmaster of Assassins from the northern city of Wargrave Abbas. He reveres Torremalku the Slayer, swift-sure bringer of death to beggar and king. The assassin moves like a black panther ready to spring; you must act quickly. Will you use a shuriken to make him drop the swordstick (turn to **239**) or a Winged Horse kick (turn to **249**)?

220

The darkness closes around you like a glove and you feel as if something terrible were about to occur. The same sixth sense makes you look behind at that moment. The ground seems to open up and a shadowy figure erupts silently out of it, like a spectre. A shaft of moonlight reveals a ninja armed with a chain, weighted at one end, and a short stick with a sickle-blade at the other, a kusarigama, emerging from a hidden pit. He darts forward and whips the weighted end of the chain around your legs and pulls hard. Your legs are yanked from under you and you crash onto your back. The other ninja leaps onto you, sitting on your belly. All this takes but an instant; you have been caught completely by surprise. Then the sickle end of the chain is in your assailant's hand and he is driving it down at you, his eyes glinting malevolently through the slit of his hood. Desperately, you try to take the wooden shaft on your forearm. Roll for a block. Your Defence is 6. If you succeed, turn to **328**. If you fail, turn to **340**.

221

In the revolution, Force-Lady Gwyneth's troops did not fight for you against the Usurper; her words to you had been, 'The Loremaster's blood does not run true in his child,' when you had failed to convince her of your worthiness. Now she bends one knee before the throne, then plants her feet firmly apart and says in her low strong voice: 'My thanks for delivering the city from the tyrant, Your Majesty. I hope that you will be as wise and just a ruler as was your father. Units of the Usurper's army still roam the city freely and there is widespread looting on the Edgeside of the city. Without law this city will lose its sinews and its strength until, at last, it will be overwhelmed by the evils of the Rift or our foes from the western Manmarch. I can restore law for you, Avenger.'

She looks you calmly in the eye, awaiting your decision. Will you invite her to step into Star Chamber (turn to **231**) or disappoint her (turn to **241**)?

The spear-head finds a gap between two scales and sinks into the monster. Black ichor spills out. The dragon roars in pain, and eyes you balefully, ignoring the boy. It lashes at you with its great ridged tail, as thick as you. If you have Acrobatics, turn to **98**. If not, your Defence is 6, as you try to vault over it. If you are hit, turn to **168**. If it misses you, turn to **192**.

Have you played Book 1: *AVENGER!* and learnt the kick Kwon's Flail? If you have, turn back to **325** and read on. If otherwise, turn to **363**.

The instant you leave the ground the Grandmaster of Shadows spins and drives a high Winged Horse kick with such speed that it takes you in the chest before you have time to accomplish the kick you had planned. You are smashed backwards. Lose 4 Endurance. If you still live, you have the presence of mind to flip in the air, and you land deftly on your feet.

'Not so bad,' he says condescendingly, 'for a student of ninjutsu.'

He starts twirling the ring about his head again and edges a little closer to you, legs apart, presenting only the side of his body to you. Will you wait until he hurls the ring at you once more when you will deliberately try to entangle your left wrist on it and drive a Leaping Tiger kick at his face (turn to **248**) or try to sweep his legs from under him with a Dragon's Tail throw (turn to **260**)?

Force-Lady Gwyneth stands stiffly erect, hand on sword-hilt, and says, 'The followers of Dama are professional soldiers but their allegiance is not to money as is the case with Antocidas the One-Eyed and his mercenaries. Nor are they liable to trip over themselves in battle as are the Usurper's troops, trained by the clerics of Nemesis, instead of by true soldiers. You have no further need of any army beyond my two thousand trained swords.'

She sits down looking around as if daring anyone to gainsay her. Turn back to **205**.

226

You are sent hurtling through the air, but you manage to flip and land lightly on your feet. Spinning round you see that the Cyclops has picked up a huge wooden club and is closing in on you, growling menacingly. You decide that to attempt a throw on so large a target would be pointless. However, you have time to throw a shuriken before engaging it. Its Defence is 6. If you have hit it, roll one die and subtract the result from the monster's Endurance of 19.

Will you now use a Leaping Tiger kick (turn to **250**) or an Iron Fist punch (turn to **262**)?

227

The Lord High Steward twitches his black cloak about him and rises to his feet: 'No ruler should be without secret informers,' he says grimly, 'We cannot boast the wiles of Vagar the Deceiver, Hermetis the Delinquent or Torremalku the Slayer but it is certain there are no others in the city capable of foiling plots against the person of Your Majesty. Foxglove has no peer when it comes to finding out what is going on amongst the dregs of society. There is much that goes on that you are shielded from due to her good work.'

He sits again. Turn back to **207**.

228

The bolt flies over your head before striking the courtyard where it shatters a slab of marble. The dragon rears its head back, preparing to snap at you with its great jaws. As it comes down, will you now drive a Leaping Tiger kick right at the tip of its nose, using Inner Force (turn to **348**), try to drive your spear into its gaping maw (turn to **294**) or hurl two shuriken as fast as you can into its mouth (turn to **330**)?

You step quickly towards Parsifal holding your hand out in fear for his life. As you step close, he whips a swordstick out from under his robe, revealing a surprisingly muscular chest as he does so. As you halt in shock a fount of acid spurts from its tip as if by magic, blinding you. This is not Parsifal you realise too late, but Mandrake, Guildmaster of Assassins from far off Wargrave Abbas, who worships Torremalku the Slayer, swift-sure bringer of death to beggar and king. In unseeing desperation you whirl your arms in a blocking motion but Mandrake knows his trade. The swordstick carries your name upon it and the Rune of Everlasting Sleep. One skilled thrust and it pierces your heart, ending your life. Mandrake kills your bodyguards and is away before the hue and cry is raised. No one has ever survived his attention.

The bolt slams into the door as you roll to the ground. You have avoided it. You come to your feet in a corridor that leads to a stairway going down. Before it, on the left, is another door. Alert for the slightest hint of a trap, you approach it. Your keen ears can detect no sound beyond. You push the door open and dart to the left, back to the wall, but there is no trap. Looking in you see an empty store room, full of robes of the priestesses of Nullaq. Then you see something that causes your heart to leap with joy. On a rack hang no less than five of the Amulets of Nullaq! You take one off the rack. The instant you touch it, your very soul is seared by a blast of ethereal energy. The pendant is utterly evil and you, as a bearer of an Amulet of Nullaq, have been tainted by its black sorcery. Lose 1 point of Inner Force, permanently; you can never have more than 4 points of Inner Force until you find redemption. Mark this and the Amulet of Nullaq on your Character Sheet. You turn and leave the room, cursing your ill fortune. You feel unclean.

Your return journey down the temple's tower is uneventful and you find lodging in an old stable for the night. You rise with the dawn and go down to the harbour. It is almost deserted. You notice a small untended single-sailed boat. Bold as brass you board it as if you owned it and cast off for the open seas. You leave the harbour unmolested and sail east toward the rising sun and the Fangs of Nadir. Turn to **79**.

231

Force-Lady Gwyneth bows low and marches through the opened door into Star Chamber. Note that she is one of your Privy Councillors on your Charter of Rulership, and then await your next supplicant. Turn to **251**.

232

Cautiously, you approach the edge of the concealed pit. Squatting down, you gingerly feel about, discovering a wooden frame disguised as turf. You lift it up to look inside. Just as you do so, a sickle-like object slices out from the pit, slashing at your legs. You are caught completely by surprise and, although you dive backwards into a handstand and then to your feet once more, your calf has been cut open. Lose 3 Endurance. If you still live, a shadowy figure erupts silently out of the pit, like a spectre. In the moonlight you can see it is another ninja. He holds a length of chain in his hands, with a wedge-shaped weight at one end and a short stick with a sickle-like blade at the other. It is a kusarigama. The ninja begins to whirl the sickle end around his head and body with frightening skill, as he edges slowly towards you. He is about to launch an attack. Will you drive a Forked Lightning kick at the ninja (turn to **268**), or use the Teeth of the Tiger throw (turn to **280**)? You decide that it will not be easy to get close enough to punch until you have seen his capability with the chain.

Whichever of the following are present — Parsifal, Golspiel, Foxglove, the Lord High Steward and/or the Demagogue — they place their closed fists on the table, indicating that they wish to speak. Anyone present who does not do so either has no advice to give or does not *wish* to give any. You may authorise any or all of your *chosen* Councillors to speak in the following order:

Parsifal: Turn to **243**.
Golspiel: Turn to **253**.
Foxglove: Turn to **263**.
The Lord High Steward: Turn to **273**.
The Demagogue: Turn to **283**.

When you have heard all you wish to hear, turn to **293**.

His face is grim: 'A Devil-Beast, foul spawn of the Dark Elves. We never knew one defiled the earth so close to us. You are a mortal of great courage and resource, Avenger — that much is evident. We were born when the world was young and we have seen mankind grow up out of the mire of creation. We know of your kind, the ninja; perhaps it is fated that you should succeed in your quest. We will aid you, for if you lay to rest a Devil-Beast you will be doing us a great service. But to pass the Fangs of Nadir into the Elemental Sea is a perilous task. Follow me, Avenger.'

You follow him deep into the forest until you come to an area where the trees are less dense but much taller. Each tree is the home of an elvan family, living on tiered tree houses. You are led to the bank of a rushing river where several boats are moored. They are of white wood, with beautifully carved swan prows.

'These are enchanted elvan boats, Mortal, and they respond to spoken commands. All you need do is tell the boat the direction you wish to travel in, and it shall bear you there. With one of these you should be able to survive even the Fangs of Nadir.' The Elf-Lord wishes you well, saying that this, the river Greenfen, runs to the Inner Sea. 'Head north, and then east to reach the Fangs,' he finishes.

You climb into one of the boats and an Elf casts you off. You command the boat forward and it sails sedately away. Turn to **252**.

235

The Lord High Steward draws himself slowly to his feet. 'The only trained soldiery in the city to be relied upon in battle are the Usurper's army and the followers of Dama. I recognise you will wish to restore the customs of your father and give the shieldmaidens their former role but two thousand shieldmaidens is not enough by itself to protect a city of this size. By choosing me as a Privy Councillor you have satisfied those followers of Nemesis who feared they would be denied your ear and their say in the governing of our city. You have nothing to fear from the Usurper's army. Remember too, that if you abolish the army as it stands now you will send four thousand onto the streets with no means of feeding their families. I'll not be responsible for what happens if you take this course.' He sits down, his jaw set firmly, deep in thought.

Turn back to **205**.

236

He thrusts the dagger at your midriff but you are ready and evade the blade. Then he sends the iron ring swinging at your head. You duck in time to see the ball of his foot hurtling towards your head, but at the last instant you slap it aside, causing him to spin round. He follows the momentum through, using the spin of his body to drive the dagger in his left hand at your chest, with devastating power. You must try to block it. Your Defence is 8. If you fail, lose 5 Endurance. If you survive, will you wait until he hurls the ring at you once more, when you will deliberately try to entangle your left wrist on it and drive a Leaping Tiger kick at his face (turn to **248**) or try to sweep his legs from under him with a Dragon's Tail throw (turn to **260**)?

237

Once again, Parsifal and Force-Lady Gwyneth are in accord. If the Force-Lady is not a Councillor she stands on the platform on which those who are not Privy Councillors may address Star Chamber; it is Parsifal who does the talking. 'The Order of The Yellow Lotus is a pestilential crew of guttersnipes given dangerous powers under the rule of the Usurper. Their effect is to prejudice your people against your rule for they breed hatred, mistrust and fear. Above all, Foxglove is not to be trusted. Abolish the Order Your Majesty; she is too dangerous to allow near your person.' Force-Lady Gwyneth nods as he finishes. Turn back to **207**.

238

You slam into the cave wall, the force momentarily stunning you. Lose 4 Endurance. You shake your head to clear away the blackness that threatens to engulf you. A growl of rage causes you to spin round. The Cyclops has picked up a massive wooden club and is swinging it at you. You duck below the scything blow and then leap to the attack. You decide that to attempt a throw on so large a target would be pointless. Will you use a Leaping Tiger kick (turn to **250**) or an Iron Fist punch (turn to **262**)?

239

In one movement you take a throwing star and send it whirling through the air at Mandrake but in the same instant the panther springs; if you miss, his blade will bury itself in your heart. Make an Attack Roll. Mandrake's Defence at this close range is only 5. If you hit him, turn to **259**. If you miss him, turn to **269**.

240

The city reacts favourably when it is announced that the army is to be strengthened by the addition of two thousand trained swords of the shieldmaidens of Dama, though there are those who wish you had banished the Orcs and Halvorcs from the city, even some who say the Usurper's army will one day rise up and cast you down from the throne even as you cast down the Usurper. Note these two member forces of the army and turn to **3**.

241

'Then the city will be without law and order,' says the Force-Lady, her voice hard with suppressed anger. 'Do not look to Dama's Temple to supply the Watch. Goodmorrow to you Avenger,' and she turns to leave. Will you calmly await the next supplicant (turn to **251**) or inform Force-Lady Gwyneth that if you command her to provide a Watch to keep order in the city then she must obey you (turn to **261**)?

242

You jump into the icy waters and dive deep, hoping to avoid the enormous Kraken. Make a Fate Roll. If Fate smiles on you, turn to **282**. If Fate turns her back on you, turn to **318**.

243

Parsifal stutters a little over what he is saying, blushing and darting nervous glances at you: 'Um, I h-hope Your Majesty will not take amiss ... um ... might it not be wise to restore the custom of your father and make the shieldmaidens of the Temple to Dama Keepers of the Watch? They enjoy a good reputation for the just keeping of law and order.' Turn back to **233**.

244

Turning about, you pad quietly past the pit's outline, without breaking your stride. A few moments after you have passed it you notice the top of the pit move slightly and a shadowy figure erupts silently out of it, like a spectre. In the moonlight, you can see it is another ninja. He carries a length of chain with a wedge-shaped weight at one end and a short stick with a sickle blade at the other. It is a kusarigama. However, he pulls up in surprise at seeing you facing him and you have time to act. Will you hurl a shuriken (turn to **292**) or use Poison Needles, if you have that skill (turn to **304**)?

Greystaff has not yet uttered a word in Star Chamber; he seems ill at ease, as if being in the chamber itself somehow tarnishes his halo. But, getting to his feet, he says, 'Now is the time, Your Majesty, to banish the filth that contaminates the airs of the city, to rid our streets once and for all of the infiltrators from the Rift, the Orcs and their cross-breed brethren, the Halvorcs. Disband the army and call on the shieldmaidens of Dama; they are fierce and doughty of heart. It is the evil ones who make possible the rule of evil in this city. Without them, the power of the Temple to Nemesis would be greatly lessened. You must act now, Sire, for the sake of your people.' He mops his brow and sits down, suddenly bowing his head. Turn back to **205**.

Deep into the sea you dive. You can feel the Elemental sucking up the sea-water beneath it as it spins upwards, and the force of the vortex plucks at you with icy fingers, but you are able to resist its pull. You come up beyond it, gulping in lungfuls of air. The small island is close now and soon you are on the shore. The island is a round circle of earth only a few hundred yards across. It is bare of vegetation and the air is cold and clammy, even though the sun beats down brightly from above. At the centre lies a cloud of mist, static and unmoving. You walk into it, and it billows about, chilling you to the bone. Then you emerge into a clearing, bounded by the mist, so that little light gets through.

A heap of skeletal remains lies piled to one side. Before it stands a Devil-Beast. It is humanoid, with great long arms that hang to the ground. Its hands are inordinately large, ending in vicious black talons. It half-squats, half-stands on two long legs – the thighs are peculiarly modified for jumping. The lifeless-looking skin is grey and warty, the head – vaguely elfin, but the nose – bulbous and misshapen. Great yellowed tusks protrude from its drooling mouth and its long thin hair is lank and matted with filth. Its eyes are dull, without intelligence, though they seem to blaze evilly with a malevolent red light. Elvan grace and beauty has been twisted into evil grotesqueness.

The Devil-Beast growls low in its throat and then nods at you. Blasts of scarlet energy lance from its eyes at you. If you have Acrobatics, turn to **302**. If not, your Defence is 6 as you try to dodge the unexpected attack. You cannot block this magical attack, either. If you are hit, turn to **264**. If you avoid it, turn to **276**.

247

Today Foxglove is wearing a dark blue woollen cloak and a small, round, dyed straw hat to match. Her face looks pale, like a corpse's – the hollows of her cheeks enhanced with purple Murex dust. Her voice is calm and grave, 'Your Majesty is in great danger. There is going to be an attempt on your life. Please leave Star Chamber immediately; summon your full bodyguard and await me in the royal bedroom. Please, please, believe me or you will surely die.' She looks imploringly at you. Turn back to **207**.

248

As you hoped, he sends the iron ring spinning towards you. Whipping your arm across its path into the hair rope causes the ring to twist around your arm. Almost simultaneously, you grab the cord and leap, lashing the ball of your foot at his face. The Grandmaster was not expecting this and your foot slams home with a crash. Note down that your opponent has lost 4 from his Endurance of 15. The force of the blow sends him flying backwards and he is forced to let go of the kyoketsu-shoze, but he flips, landing in a handstand, and continues to flip backwards to the altar. He reaches it and takes up a scabbarded ninja sword from behind the altar. As you disentangle the cord from your arm and cast it aside – it would be useless in your untrained hands – he jumps towards you again, coming to a halt some four feet in front of you. The left hand on the scabbard, the other on the hilt, poised to draw. If you have the skill of ShinRen, turn to **272**. If not, turn to **296**.

As you take up the martial stance of the Way of the Tiger, ready to unleash your kick, Mandrake lunges with the speed and skill of a champion swordsman. You try desperately to match his speed and bring your arm across to block the blade which lances towards your heart. Your Defence is 6 as you try to stop Mandrake, Guildmaster of Assassins. If you succeed in your block, turn to **47**. If you fail to deflect the blade, turn to **69**.

It swings its club at your head, but you duck and dart forward. Then you jump up and drive the ball of your foot at its throat. If you succeed and you have the skill of Yubi-Jutsu, or Nerve-Striking, you may add 2 to the damage.

HORNED CYCLOPS
Defence against Leaping Tiger kick: 7
Endurance: 19
Damage: 2 Dice

If you win, turn to **298**. If the Horned Cyclops still lives, your Defence is 7 as it tries to smash its hammer-like fist into your face. If you survive you may try an Iron Fist punch (turn to **262**) or another kick (return to the top of this paragraph).

The doors swing open once more and a huge, bulky figure waddles slowly into the Throne Room. It is Golspiel of the Silver Tongue, a merchant who owns a huge purple-draped emporium on Low End Road, near the Green. His eyes are like small shining currants in a face that shudders in time with his footfalls. His fat jowls hang down like dewlaps and his hands are like bunches of pork sausages. He bows low, breathing heavily with the effort, and says, 'Your illustrious Majesty, you are come like the Redeemer himself to deliver us from evil.'

If you have read Book 3: *USURPER!* and Golspiel gave you a piece of Red Coral and the support of his mercenaries (led by Antocidas the One-Eyed), turn to **301**. If he gave you an Amber Pendant, or if you made no dealings with him, turn to **177**. If he gave you a Jade Lotus blossom or if you have not read *USURPER!*, turn to **311**.

252

The elvan boat takes you down a meandering river, through lush greenery, and woodland filled with myriad flowers and monkeys of many colours. Soon you come out of the Forest of Fables, and the river empties into the Inner Sea. You command the boat to follow the coastline north. Soon it turns east and at last the Fangs of Nadir lie before you. They are incredible to behold. A thin strait passes between two rocky headlands that almost meet. But they crash together continually, driven by some enchantment, or perhaps the very rocks themselves are alive. The force of their meeting sends a great booming roar into the skies, and the water around the rocks heaves and surges in turmoil. You are thankful that you are not trying to pass through in an ordinary sailing boat, for you would stand no chance. You will have to time it perfectly so that the rocks are surging apart when you try to race through. Will you pass nearest to the left-hand mass of rock (turn to **48**) or to the right (turn to **62**)?

253

Golspiel's voice is at its most urgent as he says, 'I fear it would prove costly to pay the shieldmaidens of the Temple to Dama to enforce the Watch yet, clearly, something must be done before the situation becomes out of hand. May I suggest that I place my troops, under their capable and disciplined General Antocidas the One-Eyed, at your disposal Majesty. That would be enough to control the most difficult of problems at no cost to the Crown.' It is true that you have no money to pay the Watch until you have raised taxes so this may be an important consideration. Turn back to **233**.

You are a split second too slow and the bolt grazes your thigh, to slam into the door. The wound begins to burn and you realise with a thrill of horror that it is poisoned. Do you have Immunity to Poisons? If you do, turn to **266**. If not, turn to **206**.

Solstice does not bother to rise to make his address. His back is bowed, his face furrowed with lines, but his voice is soft and sweet, that of a young boy. 'Temperance, Majesty, temperance. Time will show whether your choice is wise, but I counsel against any rash move. If the city is to continue through to the end of this millennium, its people must learn to live together. I do not advise against using the shieldmaidens of Dama in the army, but I do counsel against abolishing the army as it now stands. That would leave us too weak. There are those in the city who call for the banishment of the Orcs, saying that they are the Spawn of the Rift, but history relates that the Orcs came as slaves from the Purple Mountains three centuries ago. They are citizens as much as I, perhaps more than you, Majesty.' Turn back to **205**.

Almost as soon as you have knelt down, the pit top moves up an inch and a thin sliver of steel whistles out, gleaming dully in the moonlight, arrowing towards your chest. Roll for a block. Your Defence is 7. If you succeed, you twist your body an inch or two at the last moment and the shuriken hurtles past. If you fail, it embeds itself in your shoulder and you lose 3 Endurance. If you still live, a shadowy figure erupts silently out of the pit, alerted by the cessation of footfalls when you stopped moving. It is a ninja, armed with a length of chain, with a wedge-shaped weight at one end and a short stick with a sickle blade at the other, a kusarigama. The ninja begins to whirl the sickle end around his head and body with frightening skill, as he edges slowly towards you. He is about to launch an attack. Will you drive a Forked Lightning kick at the ninja (turn to **268**), or use the Teeth of the Tiger throw (turn to **280**)? You decide that it will not be easy to get close enough to punch until you have seen his capability with the chain.

257

Greystaff, High Priest of the Temple to Avatar, and the Demagogue have discussed this matter. If either is not a Councillor then they both stand on the platform below the oval table from which those who are not members of Star Chamber may address the Council. The Demagogue tells you that the Order of the Yellow Lotus is hated by the people of Irsmuncast almost as much as the Usurper was. Greystaff delivers a homily on the subject of trust and the people's response to being trusted. He implies that having secret informers encourages people to plot treason by suggesting that you expect it; both call for the abolition of the Order. Turn back to **207**.

258

You do not dive deep enough and you are drawn up into the vortex of the Elemental as it sucks up the sea-water beneath it. You struggle to escape the watery confines of its liquid body but you are held fast and then plunged into the depths. The pressure builds up in your ears until you black out, drowned in the Elemental Sea.

259

The throwing star is unleashed with such speed and force that even the Guildmaster of Assassins is taken by surprise. It catches him in the upper arm, whirling him round and sending the swordstick bouncing away to the other end of the room. In an instant you are upon him and a second later he is dead. Though you have been using your brain rather than your body of late it has evidently not lost its speed and power. The Palace crier spreads the news of your heroic escape from death and there is great feasting in your honour. Turn to **419**.

Just as you drop into a slide, the Grandmaster of Shadows somersaults forward in the air to land behind you. As your legs scissor empty air, he twists and slices the dagger across the back of your neck, severing your spinal cord. You die instantly.

The Force-Lady does not bother to hide the contempt in her voice: 'At a price, Avenger; the treasury is empty. Without goodwill you have nothing.' Will you allow her to leave and await the next supplicant (turn to **251**) or order her to be clapped in irons in the dungeon to punish her for her temerity in addressing her Overlord so (turn to **271**)?

It tries to bring its club down on your head, but you sidestep the blow and drive your fist up at its hairy solar plexus. If you succeed and you have the skill of Yubi-Jutsu, or Nerve-Striking, you may add 2 to the damage.

HORNED CYCLOPS
Defence against Iron Fist punch: 6
Endurance: 19
Damage: 2 Dice

If you win, turn to **298**. If the Horned Cyclops still lives, your Defence is 7 as it lowers its head and tries to gore you with its horn. If you survive you may try the Leaping Tiger kick (turn to **250**) or another punch (return to the top of this paragraph).

Foxglove's beautiful face is strong and decisive. Her scarlet lips are pursed and her gaze unwavering: 'If you will allow me to send my followers into the city streets, Majesty, we will have identified and incarcerated the troublemakers by sundown. They will only need to cool their heels for a few days and the city will return to normal. As soon as that has happened I can recruit a new Watch from the people. I could hone them into an effective lawkeeping force cheaply and quickly.' She seems certain that the Order of the Yellow Lotus can stop the looting. Turn back to **233**.

264

The blasts of ruby energy lance into your body, burning you badly. Lose 6 Endurance. If you still live, you look up to see that its eyes are dull and empty, save for a gleam of malice. It gathers itself to leap, and you may hurl a shuriken as it bounds towards you. Its Defence against this is 7 and, if you hit, you may take one die from its Endurance of 14. Whether you are successful or not, it lands in front of you, talons flailing. Will you use a Forked Lightning kick (turn to **314**), a Whirlpool throw (turn to **324**) or a Tiger's Paw chop (turn to **338**)?

265

Whose advice will you act on? Will you follow the ideas of the Demagogue (turn to **275**), Force-Lady Gwyneth (turn to **285**), the Lord High Steward or Solstice (turn to **240**), or Greystaff (turn to **21**)?

266

The deadly venom courses through your blood; you sink to your knees, waves of nausea and pain flowing over you. But your years of training win over and your resistance to poison enables you to withstand its effects. After a few minutes you stand on shaking legs, groggy and dizzy. You come round in a corridor that leads to a stairway going down. Before it on the left is another door. Alert for the slightest hint of a trap, you approach it. Your keen ears can detect no sound beyond. You push the door open and dart to the left, back to the wall, but there is no trap. Looking in, you see an empty store room, full of robes of the priestesses of Nullaq. Then you see something that causes your heart to leap with joy. On a rack hang no less than five of the Amulets of Nullaq!

You take one off the rack. The instant you touch it, your very soul is seared by a blast of ethereal energy. The pendant is utterly evil and you, as a bearer of an Amulet of Nullaq, have been tainted by its black sorcery. Lose 1 point of Inner Force, permanently; you can never have more than 4 points of Inner Force until you find redemption. Mark this and the Amulet of Nullaq on your Character Sheet. You turn and leave the room, cursing your ill fortune. You feel unclean.

Your return journey down the temple's tower is uneventful and you find lodging in an old stable for the night. You rise with the dawn and go down to the harbour. It is almost deserted. You notice a small untended single-sailed boat. Bold as brass you board it as if you owned it and cast off for the open seas. You leave the harbour unmolested and sail east towards the rising sun and the Fangs of Nadir. Turn to **79**.

267

Whose advice will you take? That of Parsifal and Force-Lady Gwyneth (turn to **277**), that of the Demagogue and Greystaff (turn to **287**), that of the Lord High Steward (turn to **297**) or, by leaving the room, that of Foxglove (turn to **307**)?

268

You leap forward and drive your foot at his midriff, but he parries it with the chain. Then you snap your foot up to his head. If you succeed and you have Yubi-Jutsu, you may add 1 to the damage.

NINJA WITH KUSARIGAMA
Defence against Forked Lightning kick: 8
Endurance: 14
Damage: 1 Die + 1

If you have killed him, turn to **316**. If you hit him and he still lives, he spins and tries to whip the weighted chain across your face. Your Defence is 7 against this move. You may try a Teeth of the Tiger throw (turn to **280**), or another kick (return to the top of this paragraph).

If you missed the ninja, he sidesteps your flailing leg and wraps the chain around it. Dropping to one knee he sweeps your other leg from under you. You land heavily, sitting in the grass. Disengaging the chain, the ninja drives his chain-wrapped fist at your face, smashing you backwards. Lose 4 Endurance. If you still live, you ignore the pain and use the momentum to roll backwards onto your feet. You may attack once more. Will you try the Teeth of the Tiger throw (turn to **280**) or another kick (return to the top of this paragraph)?

269
The Guildmaster of Assassins ducks and lunges in one swift controlled motion. The throwing star shrieks wildly as its point is shattered on impact with the wall. Mandrake knows his trade well. The swordstick's blade is engraved with the name 'Avenger' and a Rune of Everlasting Sleep. It enters your heart and ends your brief reign. No one has ever survived the attention of Mandrake.

270
Your foot slams into the tip of its sensitive nose with bone-crushing force. The dragon rears back in agony, pawing at its snout, giving you time to back away. There is a bellow of rage and you see Paladin charging at the dragon, wielding his shining white sword. The dragon whips round to face him, but Paladin delivers a mighty blow and his sword slices through the dragon's scales like a hot knife through butter. Black ichor bubbles forth. The dragon rears back, roaring, and Paladin thrusts his sword into its belly. The dragon tries to escape, but Paladin's attack is relentless. With three sword-cuts he shreds one of its wings and soon it is all over. Never have you heard tell of a dragon so easily bested by one man before. At the sight of this the rest of the dragon host breaks off the attack and departs, leaving many dead dragons and men behind. Turn to **360**.

271
Gwyneth can scarcely suppress her fury. 'So you would have me imprisoned without a trial. It seems we have exchanged one tyrant for another.' Her longsword hisses from its sheath, its blade shining as if it were forged yesterday. Red

runes encircle the pommel. The monks of Kwon quail before her wrath. Will you attack her yourself (turn to **281**) or let her go (turn to **291**)?

Will you attack her yourself (turn to **281**) or let her go (turn to **291**)?

272

The Training of the Heart enables you to sense his intent. His posture and expression tells you that he plans some trickery, a device or ploy of some kind. Not wishing to take chances, you leap back. At the same instant, he draws his sword and sweeps the scabbard across in an arc. A fine mist of dust and liquids sprays out, but you are already out of range. He stares silently at you for a moment, inscrutable now. Then he lays the sword down and mutters distantly, 'In O Musubi.' You stand unmoving. It is as if you were enchanted, and a deathly hush falls in the room. The Grandmaster stares ahead, unseeing. Putting his hands together he begins to twist them around each other, making different shapes and signs. He makes nine different signs, each one punctuated by a low guttural murmur, as if he were using Inner Force.

Suddenly the room is plunged into darkness and you come out of your apathy, alert as before. The Grandmaster of Shadows has used some kind of ninja magic, something unknown to you, to create darkness. You tense and begin to circle warily, as silently as you can. It is pitch black; your enemy could be anywhere. Senses straining, you try to locate him. Your spine tingles as you think about what you are up against. This is the Grandmaster of Shadows, a master of the special skill of the ninja of the Way of the Scorpion – Innin, the skill of silent stealth or the Secret Shadow. The words above the entrance to this place come unbidden to your mind, 'Make the night your friend and darkness your cloak of invisibility.' You are at a disadvantage here, in the Grandmaster's element.

You can hear nothing; it is as if you were alone. Suddenly, your every sense is concentrated at a point in the middle of your chest. You can feel something touch you there. Will you strike out with an Iron Fist punch (turn to **332**) or slide forward into a sweeping Dragon's Tail throw (turn to **344**)?

The Lord High Steward speaks quietly and slowly so that it is almost as if you are hanging onto his every word: 'All those who seek refuge from the mob may do so in the Temple to Nemesis. I suggest that we reinstate the Usurper's Watch to identify the troublemakers and imprison them, after fair trial of course. Peace will soon be restored within the city and then we can let them go free. The Temple to Nemesis is willing to fund and raise a law-keeping force which would act impartially, not as under the Usurper's rule, and be answerable in the last resort to you, Majesty.' Turn back to **233**.

Looking through the pile of rubbish reveals only a disgusting stink, until you notice an old and battered ninja costume, presumably that of the Scorpion Ninja from the Valley of Scorpions. Rolled up into it is a small iron ring; a small black scorpion set in amber is its stone – an insignia of the ninja of the Way of the Scorpion. Pocketing it, you leave the cave and head on up the path. Note the Scorpion Ring on your Character Sheet and turn to **286**.

By pointedly ignoring the two groups of professional soldiery in the city you have antagonised them both. The Usurper's troops, no longer paid, skulk around in the city, generally up to no good. Others seek work as mercenaries in far-away lands. When the rains come in the month of Demondim and the Spawn of the Rift launch a raid against the city, the walls are unmanned. The citizen militia, lacking any great skill at arms, are cut down in the streets one stormy night by an avalanching horde of Dark Elves and Cave Trolls. Many hundreds of people are slain and the Riftspawn make off with their booty at dawn. The Temple to Nemesis chooses this moment to attempt a counter-revolution. The other factions, seeing that you cannot protect the city, do not rally to your side. Your bodyguards are slain and you are taken at last, after a valiant struggle, and broken on the wheel in sight of the Temple to Kwon.

276

The flaming blasts of ruby energy lance past your shoulder. You look up to see that its eyes are dull and empty, save for a gleam of malice. It gathers itself to leap and you may hurl a shuriken as it bounds towards you. Its Defence against this is 7 and, if you hit, you may take one die from its Endurance of 14. Whether you are successful or not, it lands in front of you, talons flailing. Will you use a Forked Lightning kick (turn to **314**), a Whirlpool throw (turn to **324**) or a Tiger's Paw chop (turn to **338**)?

277

You give the command that the Order of the Yellow Lotus is to be abolished. If previously they had been Keepers of the Watch, the position will have to be filled again, while Foxglove will have to confine herself to her duties as a priestess of Nemesis. There is no doubt that this is a popular move, but rumours of a raiding party approaching from the Rift spoil any beneficial effect this might have on the popularity of your rule. Turn to **407**.

278

The crowd files through the yawning doors into a huge vaulted chamber. You move to its edge, casually manoeuvring yourself towards a small corridor that leads away from the chamber. At the far end of the huge hall is a huge dais topped with a massive bronze idol in the shape of an enormous bloated spider. Eight huge rubies serve as its multi-faceted eyes, seeming to gleam with malevolent intelligence in the temple's gloom. Before the dais, the floor drops away into a large circular pit. A massive iron grille lies across it. A trap door has been opened in the middle of the grille. Several priestesses stand in attitudes of prayer on the dais.

The ceremony begins and the priestesses begin a keening chant; the congregation joins in, filling the temple with sound. After a time, a cage is lowered from above. Inside it, a young woman – an Elf, you think – is trembling with fear. The cage is lowered through the trap-door and the keening chant grows louder, changing in tone and content although the words are meaningless to you. Soon the cage comes up again, empty.

As the congregation falls to their knees you dart unseen into the corridor. There is a door at its end. You open it and step through into a circular room with a staircase going up at the other side. Another Elf-maiden, dark haired and golden eyed, her face wet with tears, is bound in chains and presumably is to be the next sacrifice. Beside her stands a priestess of Nullaq in red and black robes, the one you saw outside the temple, an Amulet at her neck. She stares at you in astonishment. 'How dare you,' she stutters in apoplectic rage. If you have the skill of Poison Needles, and wish to use one, turn to **290**. If not, him to **300**.

279

As you take up a martial stance and edge towards the sword-tip of the ashen-faced shieldmaiden there is the faintest whisper of movement as Parsifal moves into position beside you; then terrible pain strikes, swiftly followed by death. It was not Parsifal but an imposter, Mandrake, the Guildmaster of Assassins from far-off Wargrave Abbas who had turned a member of your bodyguard against you. No one has ever survived Mandrake's attention.

280

The ninja lashes out with the chain, trying to curl it around your legs, but you leap high in a drop-kick and hook your legs around your surprised opponent's head. Twisting savagely, you send him cartwheeling through the air. He lands badly, his neck broken, and the kusarigama buried in his chest – quite dead. Turn to **316**.

281

The battle is fierce and bloody. Only Honoric amongst all of your many foes has shown skill with the blade surpassing

that of the Force-Lady. Three monks lie dying before she succumbs, killed by a blow to her stomach that ruptures her insides. There is uproar in the Throne Room. The tumult is soon echoed in the streets of the city. A young acolyte of the monastery rushes in to say the shieldmaidens are marching on the Palace, led by the priesthood of Time. The three most powerful factions in the city are now against you and your actions have lost you the support of the common people. You are cast out of the city, an exile whose skein of destiny has become twisted and gone awry. You will have to return to the Island of Tranquil Dreams and live out your allotted span as a hermit.

282

You swim underwater for as long as you can and surface some way behind the Kraken. Looking back, you see it is crunching up the elvan boat in its beak. However, it seems not to have noticed you. You are tempted to thank Nullaq for the rank stupidity of her daughter. Suddenly a great geyser erupts beside you, and another Elemental rises up like a liquid tornado. Quickly you dive down in an attempt to swim under it. Make another Fate Roll, but subtract 2 from your Fate Modifier for this roll. If Fate is with you, turn to **246**. If Fate is against you, turn to **258**.

283

The Demagogue is quite agitated; his voice changes pitch disconcertingly. 'The people are only reacting high-spiritedly to the good news of your coronation, Your Majesty. I am sure that if I were to address the crowd from the Palace crier's podium I could persuade them of the folly of their ways. What need has Irsmuncast of oppressive Keepers of law and order? We must encourage the men and women in the street to report wrong-doings to the Palace instead.' Turn back to **233**.

284

As the spray of dust and chemicals billows outwards, you cartwheel to the side, safely out of reach. At this, the

Grandmaster of Shadows stares silently at you for a moment, inscrutable now. Then he lays the sword down and mutters distantly, 'In O Musubi.' You stand unmoving. It is as if you were enchanted, and a deathly hush falls in the room. The Grandmaster stares ahead unseeing. Putting his hands together he begins to twist them around each other, making different shapes and signs. He makes nine different signs, each one punctuated by a low guttural murmur, as if he were using Inner Force.

Suddenly the room is plunged into darkness and you come out of your apathy, alert as before. The Grandmaster of Shadows has used some kind of ninja magic, something unknown to you, to create darkness. You tense and begin to circle warily, as silently as you can. It is pitch black; your enemy could be anywhere. Senses straining, you try to locate him. Your spine tingles as you think about what you are up against. This is the Grandmaster of Shadows, a master of the special skill of the ninja of the Way of the Scorpion – Innin, the skill of silent stealth or the Secret Shadow. The words above the entrance to this place come unbidden to your mind: 'Make the night your friend and darkness your cloak of invisibility.' You are at a disadvantage here, in the Grandmaster's element.

You can hear nothing; it is as if you were alone. Suddenly your every sense is concentrated at a point in the middle of your chest. You can feel something touch you there. Will you strike out with an Iron Fist punch (turn to **332**) or slide forward into a Dragon's Tail sweep (turn to **344**)?

285

Your move to replace the army with the shieldmaidens is popular with all but the Usurper's army and others who follow Nemesis. Add 1 to your Popularity Rating and note the single force that now composes your army. Disbanding the standing army, however, causes problems. There are now four thousand jobless men and Orcs roaming the streets and unable to feed their families. Idle hands turn to no good and there is friction and violence on the streets. If the followers of Dama are Keepers of the Watch they manage to keep the situation under control (turn to **3**). If Golspiel's mercenaries run the Watch turn to **295**. If you are relying on Foxglove's Order of the Yellow Lotus to keep order turn to **305**.

<h2 style="text-align:center">286</h2>

The path leads up towards the forbidding Crags of Abandoned Hope. Soon it becomes little more than a series of footholds which appear to be little used – or, at least, anything that has been this way has not left any tracks. At last, the torrential rain ceases and the sun peeks out from behind the clouds. However, the fresh bright light serves only to highlight the barren nature of these hills. After a time, the path widens into a small flattish clearing, directly below the three gnarled crags. Then you freeze in shocked surprise; by its edge lies a seemingly innocent rock, but carved into it is a whirlpool symbol, the symbol of the god Nemesis – the god of the ninja of the Way of the Scorpion. Your senses straining, you search the surrounding rocks intently. A feeling that someone – or something – is watching you becomes overwhelming. Cold, hostile eyes are upon you. Will you ignore the feeling and climb up the crags (turn to **394**), act as if you were about to be attacked and dive for the cover of a nearby outcrop of rock (turn to **406**), or, if you have a Scorpion Ring will you hold up the ring and say, 'I am ninja, of the Way of the Scorpion, returning home from a mission given me by the Grandmaster of Shadows,' (turn to **4**), or hold up the ring and say 'I am ninja of the Scorpion, of the Island of Plenty, with messages for the Grandmaster of the ninja of the Mountains of Undying Solitude; this ring is my token of faith,' (turn to **16**)?

<h2 style="text-align:center">287</h2>

You give the command that the Order of the Yellow Lotus is to be abolished. If previously they had been Keepers of the Watch, the position will have to be filled again, while Foxglove will have to confine herself to her duties as a priestess of Nemesis. There is no doubt that this is a popular move, but rumours of a raiding party approaching from the

Rift spoil any beneficial effect this might have on the popularity of your rule. Turn to **407**.

288

The fat merchant does not appear unduly dismayed, but rather pensive. It looks as though he were about to say more. In the end he seems to decide against pushing his new Overlord and he waddles out. Turn to **331**.

289

With the speed of a striking cobra you sweep Parsifal's legs out from under him and he lands heavily on the floor. Will you attack the shieldmaiden whose sword is raised high to smite your crown (turn to **89**) or finish off your fallen victim (turn to **359**)?

290

You have a needle on your tongue in a flash as you blow hard. It slaps into her face and she utters a gasp of surprise. Then she stiffens in pain and keels over, quite dead a few seconds later. You remove the Elf-maiden's chains and she sits a moment, sobbing with relief. Quickly you snatch up the priestess's Amulet. The instant you touch it, your very soul is seared by a blast of ethereal energy. The pendant is utterly evil and you, as a bearer of an Amulet of Nullaq, have been tainted by its black sorcery. Lose 1 point of Inner Force, permanently; you can never have more than 4 points of Inner Force until you find redemption. Mark this and the Amulet of Nullaq on your Character Sheet.

Cursing your ill fortune, you turn to the Elf-maiden and to your next problem of getting you and her out, for you cannot leave her here to be sacrificed. Thinking quickly you tell her to put on the priestess's robes. She hurries to obey, pulling the cowl over her face to hide the bright elfin features. You step out into the huge chamber where the congregation is waiting expectantly for the next sacrifice to be brought out. Quickly you hurry out of the temple. The gate guards hesitate, finding it odd that a priestess should leave in the middle of worship, but they do not act. When you are safely away from the temple, the Elf leads you through the streets. Turn to **342**.

291

You have been seen to back down before Force-Lady Gwyneth. She marches out of the Throne Room with her head high and a look of contempt in her eye. The court retainers and servants will spread the word that you are a weak and vacillating Overlord. Subtract 2 from your Popularity Rating; then turn to **251**.

292

The five-bladed throwing star is whirring through the air in an instant, gleaming dully in the moonlight. It thuds into the other ninja, who staggers back. He makes no sound but plucks it from his shoulder, and throws it aside. Then he begins to whirl the sickle end of his kusarigama around his head and body with frightening skill, as he edges slowly towards you. He is about to launch an attack. Will you drive a Forked Lightning kick at the ninja (turn to **268**), or use the Teeth of the Tiger throw (turn to **280**)? You decide that it will not be easy to get close enough to punch until you have seen his capability with the chain. However, you may note that he has lost 3 from his Endurance of 14 for the shuriken wound.

293

Whose advice will you act on? Will you follow the ideas of Parsifal (turn to **303**), Golspiel (turn to **313**), Foxglove (turn to **323**), the Lord High Steward (turn to **333**) or the Demagogue (turn to **343**)?

294

The dragon's Defence is 8 as you thrust with the spear. If you are successful, turn to **384**. If not, turn to **374**.

295

Golspiel seizes upon the situation to invite many of the Usurper's soldiers to join his band of mercenaries. When he has swollen the ranks of his troops to three thousand he puts down the unrest cruelly, clapping many of the Orcs, in particular, into the city jail. Too late you realise that he has effectively wrested power from your hands, without knocking you off your throne. Resentment grows as he begins to squeeze money from your people like blood from a stone. Subtract 2 from your Popularity Rating and turn to **3**.

296

You prepare to defend yourself. He draws with lightning speed but then sweeps the scabbard across in an arc. A fine mist of dust and liquid sprays out towards your eyes. If you have the skill of Acrobatics, turn to **284**. If not, all you can do is cover your eyes. Desperately, you try to get your arm up in time.

Make a Fate Roll. If Fate smiles on you, turn to **308**. If Fate turns her back on you, turn to **320**.

297

You decide to follow the advice of the Lord High Steward and retain the services of Foxglove and the Order of the Yellow Lotus. This provokes a storm of protest but rumours of a raiding party approaching from the Rift overshadow the importance of your decision to keep the secret informers. You must, however, subtract 2 from your Popularity Rating. If that now stands at zero or below turn to **315**. If it is above zero turn to **407**.

298

The Cyclops groans weakly, dropping its club and falling to its knees. You step forward and deliver a punishing Winged Horse kick at its chin, snapping back its head and breaking its neck. The beast collapses backwards, dead. After catching your breath and tending to any of your wounds, you survey the cave.

Will you search the pile of bric-a-brac in the corner (turn to **274**) or leave the cave and move on up the path (turn to **286**)?

With the speed of a striking cobra you sweep Parsifal's legs from under him and he lands heavily on the ground and shouts at the two monks to kill you. Their loyalty to their High Grandmaster has matured over decades; their loyalty to you is a recent thing. One of them launches himself through the air attempting to use the Leaping Tiger kick on you. Will you try to block the kick (turn to **129**) or use a killing blow, chopping into the neck of the fallen Parsifal (turn to **359**)?

As you run to attack her, she steps back, and cries, 'You are no common citizen, you cursed filth!' and she gestures at you with her hands. A stream of glutinous strands, sparkling with energy, spring from her fingers and spread out like a web to engulf you. Desperately, you try to throw yourself under the web, before it grows too wide. Your Defence is 7 as you try to avoid it. You cannot block this attack. If it has struck you, turn to **350**. If you have dodged it, turn to **336**.

'My men are ready to serve you, Avenger. Ahem ... If you recall, we struck a bargain ... Enough of that for now; let me just say that I am a wealthy man who knows the vagaries of this city. It is well known that the treasury's coffers are empty; I can fill them for you. I am wise in the ways of the world and so it is my pleasure to offer myself up to you as adviser. You will find that the problems which beset your rule will be many – more than you can imagine. I have lived through the hard times of the tyrant's rule and know how to turn things to profit. Money, influence, good counsel, friends in other cities – all of these I offer. Will you take them?' He smiles, his eyes almost hidden in the creases of his cheeks. He is undoubtedly a wily fellow who seems to have made a second fortune while the Usurper was sucking the city dry. Will you invite him to step into Star Chamber (turn to **351**) or disappoint him (turn to **321**)?

You leap up into the air, execute a double somersault over the lancing flames and land lithely on your feet. You look up to see that its eyes are dull and empty, save for a gleam of malice. It gathers itself to leap and you may hurl a shuriken as it bounds towards you. Its Defence against this is 7 and, if you hit, you may take one die from its Endurance of 14. Whether you are successful or not, it lands in front of you, talons flailing. Will you use a Forked Lightning kick (turn to **314**), a Whirlpool throw (turn to **324**) or a Tiger's Paw chop (turn to **338**)?

If you will not countenance giving Force-Lady Gwyneth this position of power there is nobody else who can take charge of the templars to Dama and form a Watch at such short notice. Turn back to **293** and choose again.

Otherwise, it is the Force-Lady herself who heads the Watch, and to good effect. By sun-down order has been restored and the impartiality with which she and her shieldmaidens bring wrongdoers to justice wins you instant popularity. Add 1 to your Popularity Rating. Over the next tenday you will see that Gwyneth is able to do a difficult job well and Irsmuncast is to become one of the safer cities in the Manmarch in which to walk the streets at night, but you will have to pay a lot of gold in the form of the shieldmaidens' wages. Note these Keepers of the Watch on the Charter of Rulership and turn to **353**.

A needle is on your tongue and winging its way toward your target in an instant. It slaps into the ninja's face just below his right eye, a perfect shot. The ninja stiffens in shock. 'What trickery is this?' he gasps, plucking at the needle. 'Spiderfish venom! Curse you and the Tiger for this!' and he sinks to the ground, twitching. Perhaps it is the night wind but you thought you heard him whisper as he fell, 'But you are truly ninja.' Turn to **316**.

305

When you realise what is happening it is too late. Foxglove is a cunning and ruthless traitress. Instead of maintaining peace the Order of the Yellow Lotus fans the flames of discontent until the dark tide of counter-revolution sweeps the city like a tidal wave. After a valiant struggle you are taken and broken on the wheel in view of the Temple to Kwon.

306

He shakes his head, 'Kind though your offer is, we know nothing of the lands to the north, nor do we travel there save to visit our kin, perhaps once in a hundred years. No, it is not for the Elves to be concerned with the doings of man. You are not a creature of evil, and I wish you well. You are free to pass through our forest, but we cannot aid you.' With that they melt away into the greenery.

Shrugging your shoulders you press on through the forest. A day and a night pass uneventfully – it is as if the forest inhabitants are avoiding you, even though you move with the stealth of a panther. You rest well in any case, and you may restore 3 points of lost Endurance.

At last you emerge from the forest to stand on the shores of the Elemental Sea. A small island lies not more than half a mile out to sea; you guess this to be the one the Grandmaster of Shadows spoke of. You are a strong swimmer and the distance would be easy for you normally but between you and the island rages the Elemental Sea. It seems calm enough save where sudden geysers and great spouts of water erupt randomly and whirl along at enormous speed for a little way, back and forth, raging around like a wall of water, before subsiding into the sea once more. The sea is aptly named, for these are Water Elementals. Taking a deep breath and sending a prayer to Kwon, you dive into the water and strike out for the island.

Make a Fate Roll. If Fate smiles on you, turn to **54**. If Fate turns her back on you, turn to **74**.

307

As you step towards the door Parsifal jumps to his feet with surprising speed. Foxglove too is on her feet making a strange gesture with both hands. Will you run out of Star Chamber (turn to **149**) or wait to see what is going on (turn to **159**)?

308

A spattering of dust and chemicals lands on your arm and hood, but your eyes are safe. Instantly, you leap back as your opponent strikes, cutting at your legs. When he sees you are not blinded, he stops and stares silently at you for a moment, inscrutable now. Then he lays the sword down and mutters distantly, 'In O Musubi.' You stand unmoving. It is as if you were enchanted, and a deathly hush falls in the room. The Grandmaster stares ahead unseeing. Putting his hands together he begins to twist them around each other, making different shapes and signs. He makes nine different signs, each one punctuated by a low guttural murmur, as if he were using Inner Force.

Suddenly the room is plunged into darkness and you come out of your apathy, alert as before. The Grandmaster of Shadows has used some kind of ninja magic, something unknown to you, to create darkness. You tense and begin to circle warily, as silently as you can. It is pitch black; your enemy could be anywhere. Senses straining, you try to locate him. Your spine tingles as you think about what you are up against. This is the Grandmaster of Shadows, a master of the special skill of the ninja of the Way of the Scorpion – Innin, the skill of silent stealth or the Secret Shadow. The words above the entrance to this place come unbidden to your mind: 'Make the night your friend and darkness your cloak of invisibility.' You are at a disadvantage here, in the Grandmaster's element.

You can hear nothing; it is as if you were alone. Suddenly, your every sense is concentrated at a point in the middle of your chest. You can feel something touch you there. Will you strike out with an Iron Fist punch (turn to **332**) or slide forward into a sweeping Dragon's Tail throw (turn to **344**)?

309

He is almost powerless to defend himself against the throwing star, due to Foxglove's spell. Utterly disfigured he slumps to the floor and you finish him off with one deft chop to the neck. You know who this must be – Mandrake, Guildmaster of Assassins. Your bodyguards have hardly had time to move but now they whisk you away to your private quarters, as the Councillors, including Foxglove who looks very dazed, leave Star Chamber. Even though you have been relying more on your wits than your body of late, your reactions appear not to have suffered. Mandrake's disguise was perfect. Without Foxglove's help you might well be dead and you send her a message of thanks. Tomorrow there will be a banquet to celebrate your survival. Turn to **419**.

310

Your timing is perfect and you manage to deflect the rock without falling off the bridge. The Horned Cyclops bellows in rage; you press on towards it. It lifts another rock and sends it flying towards your head. Desperately, you try to throw yourself forward under the flying projectile. Make a Fate Roll, but you may add 1 to your Fate Modifier for this roll only. If Fate is with you, turn to **106**. If Fate deserts you, turn to **118**.

311

When you crept stealthily into the dungeons below the Palace, to surprise the Usurper, you were attacked by a Werewolf. As Golspiel stands before the throne you remember the man-beast told you that the fat merchant had sent him to slay you. You triumphed over the unnatural lycanthrope but as far as you know you may, thanks to Golspiel, have caught its disease; you may find yourself turned into a Werewolf yourself, howling at the next full moon. Will you order the monks to clap the merchant in irons in that same dungeon and force him to stand trial for High Treason tomorrow (turn to **371**), or leave the matter behind and hear what he has to say (turn to **381**)?

When you have finished, she says solemnly, 'A shame it is that you must take up a tool of Nullaq, for they are ridden with evil. I know nothing of the lands beyond the Inner Sea, nor have I heard this word, "ninja", save rumours and fables of a dreaded group of assassins that follow the Principle of Evil. But I believe your story for there is sincerity in your heart. There is little I can do to aid you. Nor should I give aid perhaps to one who follows Kwon the Redeemer. For he would lay laws and strictures upon all that is free and naked.' Her brow furrows in thought, 'But you have great courage and are of good heart. And you have done me a service I can never repay. I name you Elf-Friend, Avenger – may you enjoy great felicity.'

As her words fade, it seems as if they carried some enchantment, for you feel an uplifting wholesomeness fill your spirit. Note you are an Elf-Friend on your Character Sheet. She smiles warmly at you. 'And now I must leave, for I have much to talk of in the temple. Farewell.' She turns and walks into the white building. You enter the city proper and find an old stable to sleep in for the rest of the night. You rise with the dawn and go down to the harbour. It is almost deserted. You notice a small untended single-sailed boat. Bold as brass you board it as if you owned it and cast off for the open seas. You leave the harbour unmolested and sail east toward the rising sun and the Fangs of Nadir. Turn to **79**.

You thank Golspiel warmly. Financing and equipping the Watch for a city the size of Irsmuncast is a costly business. Golspiel is clearly a very wealthy man. The looters are quickly and brutally driven off the streets by Antocidas the One-Eyed and his mercenaries who certainly seem capable of suppressing any open hostility to your rule, but tales of bribery will begin to filter back to you over the tenday that follows. It will seem that some of the money the rich are paying to avoid being arrested on trumped-up charges might be finding its way into a corrupt Golspiel' s vast coffers. The mercenaries are to become hated by most of the people and you will be forced to depend on them heavily for protection. Note these Keepers of the Watch on the Charter of Rulership and subtract 2 from your Popularity Rating.

Turn to **353**.

314

You kick at its groin then up at its neck in a rapid one-two strike.

DEVIL-BEAST
Defence against Forked Lightning kick: 8
Endurance: 14
Damage: 1 Die + 3

If you have reduced it to 4 or less Endurance, turn to **354**. If not, it tries to grab you and bite at your throat with its razor-sharp teeth. Your Defence is 7. If you still live, will you use a Tiger's Paw chop (turn to **338**), a Whirlpool throw (turn to **324**) or another kick (return to the top of this paragraph)?

315

The people are fed up. Disillusioned with your inability to rule strongly and wisely, the general mood swings against you. Agitators whip up feeling against you and scrolls accusing you of weakness, injustice, favouritism, treachery to the people, and a list of other criticisms almost without end circulate the city. You are reading one of these scandal-mongering rags when the priests of Nemesis come for you. Nobody will lift a finger to save you. After a valiant struggle, your bodyguards are killed and you are taken to be broken on the wheel in view of the Temple to Kwon. Evil rules once more in the City of Irsmuncast nigh Edge.

316

You creep on through the night. Everything is quiet when you come to the low stone wall that surrounds the village. You slide over it silently, crouching at the other side and reaching out into the night with your senses. But everything remains still. You steal into the village itself, unseen – as far as you can tell. Some huts have lanterns outside and you avoid these pools of light like the plague. Eventually, you are standing beside the well at the centre of the village.

You climb into it and edge your way down – back to one wall, feet braced against the other. It is black as coal, and you cannot see anything save for a glimmer of yellow light below you. As you near it, you see it comes from a side tunnel set in the wall, some ten feet above the water in the well. As quietly as you can, you enter the tunnel and find yourself able to stand. The tunnel, more like an alcove in fact, ends in a wooden door which has a lantern beside it. The door is painted with a large red scorpion, rising out of a whirlpool; over the door an inscription reads 'Make the night your friend and darkness your cloak of invisibility.' You notice a small indentation where the handle should be – a circular lock. If you have a Scorpion Ring, turn to **376**. If you do not have the ring, but have the skill of Picking Locks, Detecting and Disarming Traps, turn to **388**. If you have neither of these, turn to **400**.

317

Force-Lady Gwyneth stands and says, 'The Order of the Yellow Lotus is a pestilential crew of guttersnipes given dangerous powers under the rule of the Usurper. Their effect is to prejudice your people against your rule for they breed hatred, mistrust and fear. Above all, Foxglove is not to be trusted. Abolish the Order Your Majesty; she is too dangerous to allow near your person.' Gwyneth nods as she finishes.

Turn back to **217**.

318

Something thick and slimy closes about your legs in the murky darkness of the sea. It tightens instantly, a grip far too strong for you to break. You are drawn into the Kraken's mouth where the snapping beak slices you in two. Death is instantaneous.

319

You kneel before him and, just as you pass the point of balance at which you can't rise quickly, Parsifal whips a wetly glistening swordstick from its place of concealment beneath his habit, revealing a surprisingly muscular chest as he does so. As you throw yourself sideways a fount of acid pours forth like a geyser from the tip of the swordstick, as if by magic. Your Defence against the acid is only 5. If you succeed in avoiding it turn to **369**. If not turn to **379**.

320

You are not quick enough. Burning peppers and acids seep into your eyes and you cannot open them. Desperately, you try to clear them, running backwards as you do so, but without sight you are an easy target. You manage to block the first few sword lunges by sound alone, but eventually the blade gets through, disembowelling you. As you fall, he lops off your head. You have failed.

321

The fat merchant does not appear unduly dismayed but his look hardens slightly: 'I trust you will remember our agreement concerning taxes and trading permits. I shall seek an early audience with Your Overlordship.' With that he waddles out. Turn to **331**.

322

You step inside its sweeping arms and unleash a double kick at its groin and solar plexus. If you succeed and you have the skill of Yubi-Jutsu, or Nerve-Striking, you may add 2 to the damage.

HORNED CYCLOPS
Defence against Forked Lightning kick: 7
Endurance: 19
Damage: 1 Die + 3

If you win, turn to **70**. If the Horned Cyclops still lives, it tries to bring its massive fists together on your head. Your

Defence is 7 as you try to duck. If you survive you may try a Dragon's Tail throw (turn to **346**), an Iron Fist punch (turn to **334**) or another kick (return to the top of this paragraph).

323

You ask Foxglove to take whatever measures are necessary to restore order but caution her that anyone who is locked up is to be treated well. She nods and says, 'Of course, Your Excellency,' and is gone with a rustle and a shimmer. The Order of the Yellow Lotus proves remarkably effective at locating the troublemakers and the looting subsides, but the force which Foxglove trains will never win the support of the populace; they call her 'the Succubus' and 'the Demon's whore'. The links with the Order of the Yellow Lotus are to prove most unpopular and trouble will continue to break out from time to time as the tendays pass. Note these Keepers of the Watch on the Charter of Rulership and subtract 2 from your Popularity Rating. Turn to **353**.

324

You try to grab one of its wrists and throw the stinking beast over your hip.

DEVIL-BEAST
Defence against Whirlpool throw: 6
Endurance: 14
Damage: 1 Die + 3

If you succeed, you may kick (turn to **314**) or punch the beast as it rises to its feet (turn to **338**), adding 2 to your Modifier and damage for this attack only. If you failed to throw the beast, it tries to wrap its taloned hands around your throat and choke you to death. Your Defence is 5. If you still live, you may punch (turn to **338**) or kick (turn to **314**).

325

If Parsifal, High Grandmaster of the Temple to Kwon, is a Privy Councillor, turn to **223**. If not, read on. You have just returned from prayer in the Temple to Kwon, having sought the guidance of the Redeemer and found only empty silence, when Foxglove arrives at the Palace and craves audience. If you call your bodyguard close and give the order to bring her to you in your study turn to **335**. If you tell her never to call on you at the Palace uninvited turn to **345**.

326
She nods slowly, 'So be it. I do not believe you have evil intent for your heart is good. I am forever in your debt and may you find every success in your endeavour, whatever it may be. Farewell.' You watch as she turns and walks into the white building of the temple. You enter the city proper and find an old stable to sleep in for the rest of the night. You rise with the dawn and go down to the harbour. It is almost deserted. You notice a small untended single-sailed boat. Bold as brass you board it as if you owned it and cast off for the open seas. You leave the harbour unmolested and sail east toward the rising sun and the Fangs of Nadir.

Turn to **79**.

327
Today Foxglove is wearing a dark blue woollen cloak and a small, round, dyed straw hat to match. Her face looks pale, like a corpse, the hollows of her cheeks enhanced with purple Murex dust. Her voice is calm and grave, 'Your Majesty is in great danger. I cannot speak about it now, but if you will give me private audience later I shall reveal how useful the Order of the Yellow Lotus is to you. To do so now, here, would be to put Your Majesty at grave risk. So I beg you not to disband the Order of the Yellow Lotus.' She looks imploringly at you as she finishes her speech.

Turn back to **217**.

328
At the last moment you get your arm across, and the wooden shaft slams against your iron sleeves with a crack, the blade stopping dead, inches from your chest. Your opponent leans onto it, forcing it down. Desperately, you try to hold him back, sweat breaking out on your forehead as you exert all

your strength to keep the blade away from you. But you cannot keep the blade away for ever – his weight is forcing it slowly down. You drive your right fist up at your assailant's face, a short-snapped Iron Fist, trying to knock him off you. Make an Attack Roll. The ninja's Defence is 7. If you use Inner Force you may add 2 to your Attack Roll. If you succeed, turn to **352**. If you fail, turn to **364**.

329

Without warning you explode into action, sailing across the room with both legs cocked as Parsifal whips a wetly glistening swordstick from its place of concealment beneath his habit, revealing a surprisingly muscular chest as he does so. He moves with incredible speed in reaction to your attack but, caught almost unawares, his Defence against your kick is only 6. If your attack succeeds turn to **339**. If you fail turn to **349**.

330

The shuriken bury themselves in the dragon's sensitive tongue and palate; you will not be able to retrieve them. It pulls up short in pain, giving you time to dive aside. There is a bellow of rage and you see Paladin charging at the dragon, wielding his shining white sword. The dragon whirls around to face him, but Paladin delivers a mighty blow and his sword slices through the dragon's scales like a hot knife through butter. Black ichor bubbles forth. The dragon rears back roaring and Paladin thrusts his sword into its belly. The dragon tries to escape but Paladin's attack is relentless. With three sword-cuts he shreds one of its wings and soon it is all over. Never have you heard tell of a dragon so easily bested by one man before. At the sight of this the rest of the dragon host breaks off the attack and departs, leaving many dead dragons and men behind. Turn to **360**.

331

The doors are flung wide again and a strange gawky figure in a tatty yellow robe which flaps loosely round his skinny knees stalks in. It is the Demagogue, the mob orator who has captured the imagination of the common people. The dark eyes, separated by the most monumental nose you have ever seen, sparkle with a strange fire. He stops before the throne and launches into a harangue before remembering himself; then he throws himself energetically to his knees:

'Great Overlord, Avenger, I greet you as the beneficent ruler who will restore the birthright of the people.' The look in his eye is close to adoration as he springs to his feet and begins to speak excitedly. 'This fair city may become one of the most priceless jewels known to men. With the people behind you, all things become possible: new buildings, new worth, health and wealth for all. A city famed amongst the far flung races of Orb. With the support of the people your reign will pass into the annals of the sages of history as the age of enlightenment. I hold the key to this support, Avenger, your most humble servant and representative of the people, who are the lifeblood of Irsmuncast.'

He pauses for breath and you decide to pass judgement before he begins another flow of fine oratory. Will you ask the Demagogue to step into Star Chamber (turn to **391**) or disappoint him (turn to **401**)?

332
You snap your fist forwards but all it connects with is the sword's scabbard which clatters to the ground. You realise the Grandmaster had the scabbard balanced on the end of his sword to confuse you as to his position. Suddenly there is a rush of air, and a sharp pain as a sword bites into the side of your thigh. Lose 6 Endurance. If you still live, you know he is in front of you now. Will you unleash a high Winged Horse kick at head-height (turn to **356**) or a low kick, driving the ball of your foot at a point about three feet off the ground in front of you (turn to **368**)?

333
The Lord High Steward stalks out of the chamber to make arrangements for the reconstitution of the Usurper's Watch, tactfully passing over some of the most hated officers. His tactics are effective and the looting stops before dusk but the

city seems to go into a state of shock when it realises that after the revolution the followers of Nemesis are still able to oppress. You let it be known that the Lord High Steward is accountable to you and he, at least in public, acknowledges this, but you are to witness demonstrations and stone-throwing beginning a few days later. Note the Temple to Nemesis as Keepers of the Watch on the Charter of Rulership and subtract 2 from your Popularity Rating. Turn to **353**.

334

As it tries to gore you with its horn you drop to one knee and try to drive a reversed Iron Fist up into its misshapen face. If you succeed and you have the skill of Yubi-Jutsu, or Nerve-Striking, you may add 2 to the damage.

HORNED CYCLOPS
Defence against Iron Fist punch: 6
Endurance: 19
Damage: 1 Die + 3

If you win, turn to **70**. If the Horned Cyclops still lives it tries to hammer you into the ground with one of its huge fists. Your Defence is 7 as you dive aside, if you survive you may try a Dragon's Tail throw (turn to **346**), a Forked Lightning kick (turn to **322**) or another punch (return to the top of this paragraph).

335

To your surprise Foxglove is today wearing white – a short jacket and breeches – but with black boots. Her hair is piled up on her head and the face-paint she wears, though alluring, is no more than might be worn by a young acolyte serving in the chapel to the All-Mother. She bows low and you ask her to sit. She begins: 'I have learned from my secret informers things which may be of interest to you, Majesty.' You nod and she goes on, 'We have found out that the price of half a king's ransom lies on your head; that one Mandrake, Guildmaster of Assassins in the far-off city of

Wargrave Abbas, attempted to assassinate you.' She mispronounces the city's name but what she says is true enough. You nod again. 'He has left Wargrave; the Guildmaster who conducts the services in honour of Torremalku the Slayer is an imposter. Mandrake is searching for you, Overlord.'

'Is there anything more?' you ask.

'Yes, we have identified certain agitators stirring up feeling against you; they won't be giving any more trouble.'

'I hope they have been dealt with fairly?' you ask.

'Of course,' says Foxglove, but her smile suggests otherwise. The evidence she brings, however, shows that she has got the right men. She takes her leave and you ponder the news about Mandrake and the worth of the Order of the Yellow Lotus. Turn to **365**.

336

You roll under the streaming webs and come up straight into a flying Winged Horse kick. Your foot takes the priestess in the chin and she falls back, out like a light. You remove the Elf-maiden's chains and she sits a moment, sobbing with relief. Quickly you snatch up the priestess's Amulet. The instant you touch it, your very soul is seared by a blast of ethereal energy. The pendant is utterly evil and you, as a bearer of an Amulet of Nullaq, have been tainted by its black sorcery. Lose 1 point of Inner Force, permanently; you can never have more than 4 points of Inner Force until you find redemption. Mark this and the Amulet of Nullaq on your Character Sheet.

Cursing your ill fortune, you turn to the Elf-maiden and to your next problem of getting you and her out, for you cannot leave her here to be sacrificed. Thinking quickly, you tell her to put on the priestess's robes. She hurries to obey, pulling the cowl over her face to hide the bright elfin features. You step out into the huge chamber where the congregation is waiting expectantly for the next sacrifice to be brought out. Quickly you hurry out of the temple. The gate guards hesitate, finding it odd that a priestess should leave in the middle of worship, but they do not act. When you are safely away from the temple, the Elf leads you through the streets.

Turn to **342**.

337

Greystaff, High Priest of Avatar, and the Demagogue have discussed this matter. If either is not a Councillor then they both stand on the platform below the oval table from which those who are not members of Star Chamber may address the Council. The Demagogue tells you that the Order of the Yellow Lotus is hated by the people of Irsmuncast almost as much as was the Usurper. Greystaff delivers a homily on the subject of trust and the people's response to being trusted. He implies that having secret informers encourages people to plot treason by suggesting that you expect it; both call for the abolition of the Order.

Turn back to **217**.

338

You bring both your hands together in a double chop aimed at both sides of its neck.

DEVIL-BEAST
Defence against Tiger's Paw chop: 7
Endurance: 14
Damage: 1 Die + 3

If you have reduced it to 4 or less Endurance, turn to **354**. If not, it tries to rip open your stomach with a taloned hand. Your Defence is 6. If you still live, you can use a Forked Lightning kick (turn to **314**), a Whirlpool throw (turn to **324**) or another double-chop (return to the top of this paragraph).

339

You were right to attack; your foe is a *young* man – certainly not Parsifal. By chopping the heel of one foot downwards and extending the other leg you succeed in hitting his arm and head simultaneously. The swordstick clatters away to the end of the room. If Foxglove has revealed to you in private conversation that Parsifal was already dead, turn to **11**. If not, read on.

You look grimly down at the man you have disarmed and knocked to the floor and recognise Mandrake, Guildmaster of Assassins, from far-off Wargrave Abbas who worships Torremalku the Slayer, swift-sure bringer of death to beggar and king. Yet it is the assassin's death which is swiftly executed in the confessional room. Before he can recover from your stunning attack you finish him off with a chop to the neck. Your reactions have not suffered even though you have been relying more on your wits than your body of late. Mandrake's disguise was perfect. Tomorrow there will be a banquet to celebrate your survival. Turn to **419**.

340

You try to intercept the sickle blade but it is too fast for you. It thuds into your shoulder sending a hot wave of agony across your body. You gasp at the shock. Lose 6 Endurance. If you still live, the ninja rips the kusarigama out and drives the blade at you once more, but this time you are ready. At the last moment, you get your arm across and the wooden shaft slams against your iron sleeves with a crack, the blade stopping dead inches from your chest. Your opponent leans onto it, forcing it down. Desperately, you try to hold him back, sweat breaking out on your forehead as you exert all your strength to keep the blade away from you. But you cannot keep the blade away for ever – his weight is forcing it slowly down. You drive your right fist up at your assailant's face, a short snapped Iron Fist, trying to knock him off you. Make an Attack Roll. The ninja's Defence is 7. If you use Inner Force you may add 2 to your Attack Roll. If you succeed, turn to **352**. If you fail, turn to **364**.

341

Your army is not yet ready to embark on a campaign against the Spawn of the Rift and so you order them to look to the defence of the walls in case of attack. When the black tide crosses the River of Beasts in sight of the watch-towers your people are ready. The fighting is bloody but the Dark Elves are repulsed – thankfully before the Cave Trolls, under cover of huge siege machines covered with damp hides, can undermine the foundations of the city walls. The attacking forces withdraw to regroup, but it is only the calm before the storm. Turn to **119**.

342

She leads you through a marble archway into a walled enclave. Here it is quiet and peaceful, away from the hubbub of the city itself. Still without a word, she takes you to a spacious courtyard where flowers and trees flourish in a riotous display of natural greenery. A simple white building rests at its centre. Restful music fills the air. She turns to you and speaks, in honeyed tones, 'I cannot thank you enough for your aid, Mortal. Your skills are strange to me but I do not believe you are a follower of evil gods.' She waits for you to speak, but when you do not she continues, her lilting voice caressing your ears. 'My name is Lithuel. This is a small temple to Tanajla, Free Spirit of Creation and Guardian of Elfdom. I will be safe here now. The vile reverencers of that – that abomination would have this place razed to the ground but they cannot, so they content themselves with one or two of our people whenever they can. And we are powerless to protest. Oh, we protest in the Council, but our voice is as a leaf in the wind here on the Isle of Thieves.' She pauses and then adds, 'Who are you Mortal, that would save one such as I, yet have need of an Amulet of Nullaq?'

Will you tell her your tale (turn to **312**) or wish her well and say that you cannot tarry (turn to **326**)?

343

From a discreet position behind the windows of the royal balcony you watch as the Demagogue mounts the Palace crier's podium in the centre of Palace Road to make his impassioned appeal to the people to stop the looting. However, the looting continues on into the night. So the Demagogue stays up, walking the streets, and beseeching the people to behave with dignity. The morning sun dawns on a tranquil city. Your move to let the Demagogue organise a Watch from the common people is popular but misguided. Add 1 to your Popularity Rating.

Public order suffers and you cannot justify convening Star Chamber for other matters. The Halls of Justice stand disused. After a few tendays, reports come in that followers of Vagar the Deceiver, thieves and vagabonds, are journeying north from Greyguilds-on-the-Moor to take rich pickings. It is soon unsafe to walk the streets at night and order collapses when widespread looting begins again on the poorer Edgeside of the city. You will have to follow the advice of one of your other Councillors and form a new Watch. Turn back to **293** and choose again.

344

As you drop, the scabbard falls on top of you, and then a sword parts the air where you were just standing. You realise the Grandmaster had balanced the scabbard on the end of his sword to confuse you as to his position. However, you have the better of him this time, for your feet sweep out, knocking his legs from under him. You hear a gasp of surprise and then the sound of someone vaulting away. Then the lights flare up unexpectedly, and you are momentarily blinded. Eyes narrowed against the glare, you can just make out your opponent, about fifteen feet away, about to hurl his sword at you like a spear. Do you have the skill of Arrow Cutting? If you do, turn to **380**. If not, turn to **392**.

345

Two days after Foxglove's visit to the Palace you hear reports that certain agitators are spreading lies about you and turning people's hearts against you. They are suggesting that you do not need the advice of your Councillors but seek instead to impose your foreigner's ways on the city. Subtract 1 from your Popularity Rating. Turn to **365**.

346

You slide forward and hook your feet around one of its tree-like legs. You twist rapidly but the beast is too heavy, rooted to the ground like a rock, and you are unable to trip it. It laughs evilly and kicks out at you. You try to roll aside but its massive foot takes you in the chest, winding you and cracking a rib. The blow hefts you off the ground and sends you flying backwards several feet where you collapse in a heap, gasping in pain. Lose 6 Endurance. If you still live, you have just enough time to spring to your feet to face it as it lumbers towards you again. Will you try a Forked Lightning kick (turn to **322**) or an Iron Fist punch (turn to **334**)?

347

The Lord High Steward twitches his black cloak about him and says, 'No ruler should be without secret informers. We cannot boast the wiles of Vagar the Deceiver, Hermetis the Delinquent or Torremalku the Slayer but certain it is that there are no others in the city capable of foiling plots against the person of Your Majesty. Foxglove has no peer when it comes to finding out what is going on amongst the dregs of society. There is much that goes on that you are shielded from due to her good work,' and he sits again. Turn back to **217**.

348

The dragon's Defence is 7 as you leap up and drive your foot at its snout, uttering a guttural cry as the Inner Force wells up inside you. If you hit the dragon, turn to **270**. If not, turn to **180**.

349

You are right to attack; your foe is a *young* man – it surely cannot be Parsifal. By chopping the heel of one foot downward and extending the other leg you attempt to strike his arms and his head, to disarm him and knock him to the floor, but your aim is off and as your foot smashes into his face he has struck with the speed of a panther. This is not Parsifal you realise with certainty too late, but Mandrake, Guildmaster of Assassins, from far-off Wargrave Abbas who worships Torremalku the Slayer, swift-sure bringer of death to beggar and king. He knows his trade well; the swordstick's blade carries the name 'Avenger' and a Rune of Everlasting Sleep. The tip scores your chest ending your brief reign at a stroke. Mandrake is gone long before your body is discovered in a chest of sacred vestments. Nobody has ever survived the attention of Mandrake.

350

As you hit the floor in a roll, a spray of sticky strands engulfs you and you are neatly trussed up in seconds. The web is burning with energy that crackles through you before it is expended. Lose 4 Endurance. You find yourself unable to move, stuck fast to the web that covers you. If you have the skill of Feigning Death, turn to **362**. If you do not, turn to **372**.

351

'I thank you, Your Majesty. I shall serve you well.' He waddles off, puffed up with his own importance even beyond the size of his body. Note that he is one of your Privy Councillors on your Charter of Rulership and turn to **331**.

352

You drive your fist into your opponent's face using all your martial skills to generate power from such short range. There is an audible crack as his head snaps back and he is propelled backwards. He falls onto his back and rolls over onto his feet, as you spring erect. The ninja begins to whirl the sickle end around his head and body with frightening skill, as he edges slowly towards you. He is about to launch an attack. Will you drive a Forked Lightning kick at the ninja (turn to **268**), or use the Teeth of the Tiger throw (turn to **280**)? You decide that it will not be wise to get close enough to punch until you have seen his capability with the chain.

353

The business of Star Chamber is done for today. You dine in peace, alert for any sound of mayhem near the Palace but the disturbances are happening out of earshot. At tomorrow's session the real tasks of policy-making will begin.

When you awake, the stillness of the Palace reminds you of how alone you are, how far away from your people in the bustling streets outside. The servants treat you with every respect as you don the cloth-of-gold robe that is worn by the Overlord of Irsmuncast when he attends the Council of Star Chamber. The Master of the Chamber in his emerald robes stands by as you break fast and suggests a series of questions of outstanding importance be placed on the agenda for today's session. If you have ordered Golspiel the merchant to stand trial, turn to **65**. If not you enter Star Chamber, together with the Master of the Chamber, at the appointed hour and greet your Privy Councillors. Turn to **75**.

354

The Devil-Beast bounds backwards on its powerful legs, howling in pain. It crouches, slavering, badly wounded. Then it waves its hand and the pile of skeletal remains begins to animate before your very eyes. Your scalp crawling, you watch as a human skeleton assembles itself from the heap of bones and clatters toward you, its joints creaking and jaws snapping. Summoning your resolve, you leap forward and drive a Winged Horse kick at the undead thing.

ANIMATED SKELETON
Defence against Winged Horse kick: 6
Endurance: 10
Damage: 1 Die + 1

If you have defeated it, turn to **366**. If not, it tries to batter you with its bony fists. Your Defence is 7. If you still live, you drive another Winged Horse kick at its grinning skull. Fight on as above.

355

Force-Lady Gwyneth is a battle-hardened veteran and a seasoned strategist. She protests that to leave the safety of the walls and march to the Rift would be folly, but she realises that she must bow to the wishes of the people. The forces of evil draw apart as if fleeing but her troops are caught in a deathly embrace when they surge together once more. The army is destroyed and the Force-Lady with it. Now nothing can stop the black tide from engulfing the city and all who live there.

356

Your kick meets only with empty air. Then a sword is driven upwards to puncture your stomach and on into your vitals. You die coughing in a pool of blood and viscera.

357

Whose advice will you take — that of Parsifal and Gwyneth (turn to **367**), that of the Demagogue and Greystaff (turn to **377**), that of the Lord High Steward (turn to **387**) or, by summoning her to your study, that of Foxglove (turn to **397**)?

358

You are left alone in the Banqueting Hall and the rattle of armour alerts you as the messenger enters. He is a very tall man, about six and a half feet, and seems almost as broad. His dark, craggy face is disfigured by a purple scar running from his receding hairline to his ear and he sports a gold eye-patch. He wears scratched and supple cuir bouilli armour, the mark of his trade, and for some reason the servants have allowed him to bring his bastard sword into your presence, but he spreads his hands, palms down, in a gesture of peace and kneels before you. 'My master, Golspiel, has asked me to say that he wishes to make a donation of ten talents to the treasury, Your Majesty. When he is at liberty he will deliver the gold to you within the day.' A talent is the weight of a man in pure gold. Golspiel's messenger – Antocidas the One-Eyed – is offering you an absolute fortune. Golspiel must be one of the richest men alive. If you accept, the treasury will be able to support your rule. Will you tell Antocidas that Golspiel will be set free forthwith (turn to **125**) or say that no-one in the city is above your law (turn to **135**)?

359

One blow to the neck ends your victim's life. The body is muscular and young. You have killed an imposter and you recognise it to be Mandrake, Guildmaster of Assassins, from far-off Wargrave Abbas. No-one has ever before survived his attention. The bodyguard forced to betray you by the Guildmaster commits suicide, unable to live with dishonour. Later there will be feasting and celebration in honour of your survival.

Turn to **419**.

360

When things are calmer Paladin walks up to you, his arm around the shoulders of his son. 'I cannot thank you enough for the life of my son, stranger,' he says. 'You acted with great courage and unselfishness. Now I am forever in your debt. How can I repay you?'

He bows before you. Will you ask him for an Amulet of Nullaq (turn to **410**) or tell him who you are and what you seek to do (turn to **158**)?

361

Your vision blurs. Solstice seems to disappear and then reappear before you. Wordless, the High Priest of the Temple to Time walks slowly towards the Council Room as if troubled by a wasting disease. Note that he is one of your four Privy Councillors on your Charter of Rulership. If you have now chosen all four, turn to **13**. Otherwise, turn to **109**.

You sink into a meditative trance almost instantly, curbing your racing mind and your bodily functions. You slow down your heartbeat to an imperceptible rate to appear as if dead. Dimly, as if in a dream, you hear someone saying, 'Dead so soon – a shame, there will be no sport with this one!' Then, there is another word, unintelligible, and the web dissolves as quickly as it was created. You surge up out of your trance into life, and leap up. The priestess steps back in utter amazement and you drive a Winged Horse kick at her head. Your foot takes the priestess in the chin and she falls back, out like a light. You remove the Elf-maiden's chains and she sits a moment, sobbing with relief. Quickly you snatch up the priestess's Amulet. The instant you touch it, your very soul is seared by a blast of ethereal energy. The pendant is utterly evil and you, as a bearer of an Amulet of Nullaq, have been tainted by its black sorcery. Lose 1 point of Inner Force, permanently; you can never have more than 4 points of Inner Force until you find redemption. Mark this and the Amulet of Nullaq on your Character Sheet.

Cursing your ill fortune, you turn to the Elf-maiden and to your next problem of getting you and her out, for you cannot leave her here to be sacrificed. Thinking quickly you tell her to put on the priestess's robes. She hurries to obey, pulling the cowl over her face to hide the bright elfin features. You step out into the huge chamber where the congregation is waiting expectantly for the next sacrifice to be brought out. Quickly you hurry out of the temple. The gate guards hesitate, finding it odd that a priestess should leave in the middle of worship, but they do not act. When you are safely away from the temple, the Elf leads you through the streets. Turn to **342**.

363

On this day you pray in the Temple to Kwon, seeking the guidance of the Redeemer and finding only empty silence. Instead you are greeted by Parsifal who invites you to walk with him.

The temple and adjoining monastery stand in a park. As

you cross the grounds, Parsifal begins to speak. 'Know it is an honour to serve as your Privy Councillor, Overlord. Know also the demands of rulership do not supersede the demands of the spirit. As your senior in the temple, it is on me to see to your continued development – and, even, your training. I hope only that my aged self can do justice for our youthful champion.'

You come to an area of cleared dirt, used for sparring, and Parsifal drops into a martial stance. His muscles have weakened but they hold memory within. Parsifal moves in a manner you have never seen: he spins to the right on his left foot, presenting his back to you, and whips his right foot round and up like a ball and chain. You step back before it can connect with your head and he gestures for you to duplicate the kick. He calls it Kwon's Flail, and though his tutelage is imperfect, you see the manoeuvre has the potential to be more powerful even than the kicks which you use. Note it on your Character Sheet as a new kick you have learnt.

Later you have graciously taken your leave of the High Grandmaster and returned to the Palace. You are informed that Foxglove has arrived and craves audience. If you call your bodyguard close and give the order to bring her to you in your study turn to **335**. If you tell her never to call on you at the Palace uninvited turn to **345**.

364

You catch your opponent on the chin, but the blow is not powerful enough to be effective; there is not enough distance or leverage for you to get power behind it. The strength fails in your arm and the blade comes crashing down to bury itself in your neck. Red spray fountains upward and you die, gurgling and choking in your own blood.

365

The third session of Star Chamber takes place on a dreary and grey afternoon. Messages threatening that your days on the throne are numbered are thrown into the Palace gardens and brought to you by a servant dripping with rain. The culprits escape the Palace guard and no-one can describe them. Will you order the random arrest of fifty people every day until the culprits are found or handed over to you (turn to **375**), or ignore the incident (turn to **385**)?

366

The skeleton collapses in a heap of shattered bones, never to rise again. The Devil-Beast still crouches before you, barely able to move, but you can see as you look up from the skeleton that its eyes are burning with red light once more. You have no time to do anything but throw yourself to the floor. Your Defence is 6, and you cannot block this magical attack. If you avoid it, turn to **378**. If not, turn to **390**.

367

You give the command that the Order of the Yellow Lotus is to be abolished. If previously they had been Keepers of the Watch, the position will have to be filled again, while Foxglove will have to confine herself to her duties as a priestess of Nemesis. There is no doubt that this is a popular move, but rumours of a raiding party approaching from the Rift spoil any beneficial effect this might have on the popularity of your rule. Turn to **59**.

368

Your foot slams home with a crack. You can hear a grunt of pain and the sound of a man vaulting backwards out of range. You may note that the Grandmaster has lost 3 from his Endurance of 15. Then the lights flare up unexpectedly, and you are momentarily blinded. Eyes narrowed against the glare, you can just make out your opponent, about fifteen feet away, about to hurl his sword at you like a spear. Do you have the skill of Arrow Cutting? If you do, turn to **380**. If not, turn to **392**.

369

As soon as your knees hit the floor you fling yourself sideways, then pivot on your hand and, as the acid spurts past, you unleash a Winged Horse kick which knocks your opponent, stunned, to the matting. Before he can recover, you deliver a crushing blow to the side of his neck which kills him outright. If Foxglove has revealed to you in private conversation that Parsifal was already dead, turn to **399**. If not, read on.

You can see this is not Parsifal but Mandrake, Guildmaster of Assassins, from far-off Wargrave Abbas. Even though you have been relying more upon your wits than your body of late, your reactions have evidently not suffered. Mandrake's disguise was perfect. Tomorrow there will be a banquet to celebrate your survival. Turn to **419**.

370

The climb down is not easy and takes some time, but the Cyclops does not notice you – the wind frustrates even its obviously keen sense of smell. It remains at the chasm's edge, casting about for the victim its brain tells it should be there. You reach the pathway safely, above the cave, and head on upwards. Turn to **286**.

371

You order Golspiel of the Silver Tongue to attend the Halls of Justice on Shieldbearers' Row at noon-tide tomorrow, there to answer the charge of High Treason against the person of Avenger I, Overlord of Irsmuncast nigh Edge. Two grey-clad monks step forward and take Golspiel by either arm. 'You cannot do this to me, Your Overlordship. Evil perverted our actions but now I have seen the light. You need my help, Avenger … You will regret this, I'll, I'll –' He is still blustering as they haul him off to the dungeons and there is a low ripple of applause from the courtiers. Golspiel is evidently not a popular man. Note that the merchant will stand trial and turn to **331**.

372

Desperately you struggle to break free, but your bonds are unnaturally strong, enchanted as they are, and you only manage to enmesh yourself further. The priestess walks up to you. 'So you would slay me and rescue Lithuel! How revoltingly noble of you, but so, so foolish,' and she laughs cruelly. She raises her arms above your head and gestures again, her eyes wild and staring. A cloud of impenetrable blackness billows from her hands to roll over you. She has cast the Breath of Nullaq spell, turning your lungs to water. You drown in minutes, threshing on the dry stone floor.

373
If any of the following are present – Parsifal, Golspiel, Force-Lady Gwyneth, the Lord High Steward or the Demagogue – they place their closed fists on the table, indicating that they wish to speak. Anyone present who does not do so either has no advice to give or does not *wish* to give any. You may authorise any or all of your *chosen* Councillors to speak in the following order:

Parsifal: Turn to **383**.
Golspiel: Turn to **393**.
Force-Lady Gwyneth: Turn to **403**.
The Lord High Steward: Turn to **413**.
The Demagogue: Turn to **5**.

When you have heard all you wish to hear, turn to **15**.

374
Your spear scrapes across one of its huge fangs harmlessly and the dragon's jaws close about your midriff. You are bitten in two and killed instantly.

375

Your bizarre and tyrannical act fills the jails within three days and all you have done is turn the people against your harsh, despotic rule. The followers of Nemesis rise up against you and no-one lifts a finger to stop the counter-revolution. Your bodyguards are slain and after a valiant struggle you are taken and broken on the wheel within sight of the Temple to Kwon. The rule of the city returns to evil.

376

It seems that the ring will fit perfectly into the door's lock. You insert the amber stone into place. To your excitement there is a click and the door slides open, to reveal a dimly lit corridor stretching away into darkness. Cautiously you step in. The floor and ceiling are polished wood – clean and simple. The wails are of sculpted stone. Carven gargoyles and demonic forms surge out, as if to bite and snap at those that walk this corridor.

Without a sound you glide on down the straight devil-lined corridor, senses alert, your heart beating rapidly. You are stealing into a veritable pit of scorpions. Death lurks, ready to pounce upon you, like a wolf-spider on its prey. In the dim light, it seems the sculpted faces and figures mock you silently; as you pass them your spine tingles in anticipation – you half expect them to roar into life and devour you.

After a time, the corridor bends to the right. As quiet as the void you pause, feet apart, and crouch. Carefully you look out and down the corridor. About twelve feet away a figure stands, another ninja guard, beside a door. His back is to you. A sword is strapped to his back. He stands in an attitude of relaxation, yet is unmoving. Will you creep forward and garrotte the sentry (turn to **412**) or hurl a shuriken at his head from the corner (turn to **8**)?

377

You give the command that the Order of the Yellow Lotus is to be abolished. If previously they had been Keepers of the Watch, the position will have to be filled again, while

Foxglove will have to confine herself to her duties as a priestess of Nemesis. There is no doubt that this is a popular move, but rumours of a raiding party approaching from the Rift spoil any beneficial effect this might have on the popularity of your rule. Turn to **59**.

378

The bolt of energy flashes past over your head. You pick yourself up off the floor and approach the Devil-Beast which cowers before you. You are filled with revulsion. A single Tiger's Paw chop finishes the creature off and it slumps to the ground, dead. Immediately, the mist dissipates and, as the sun's rays play upon the Beast's body, it begins to shrivel up until nothing is left but ashes. Resting atop the ashes is a Sceptre of gold, inlaid with many gems. Embossed on the mace-like head is a finely carved golden hippogriff. Beside the Sceptre lies a glowing green gem, the Orb. It is not as large as you expected, perhaps the size of an eye. At last, you have found that which you have sought. A great weariness comes over you, for you have battled long and mightily to find these things. You reach down and pick them up. Suddenly everything around you goes white and misty. Turn to **420**.

379

You are too slow; the spurting acid bathes your face, blinding you. You realise with certainty that it is not Parsifal, but Mandrake, the Guildmaster of Assassins from far-off Wargrave Abbas. In unseeing desperation you whirl your arms in a blocking motion but Mandrake knows his trade. The swordstick carries your name upon it and the Rune of Everlasting Sleep. One skilled thrust and it pierces your heart ending your life. Mandrake is gone long before your body is discovered in a chest of sacred vestments. No-one has ever survived his attention.

380

Momentarily blinded as you are your reflexes take over and you deflect the flying blade with your iron sleeves. The ring of steel on steel echoes around the chamber and the sword embeds itself in the wooden flooring where it quivers as if alive. Your vision clears. A short wooden stick drops out of the master ninja's sleeve into his hand and he darts forward raising it to strike at your shoulder without a sound. Will you try to block it (turn to **404**) or allow him to hit you and drive a Leaping Tiger kick into his face while his guard is down (turn to **416**)?

381

'I did not believe it possible to defeat the Usurper in the fastness of his Palace, but you have shown me the error of my ways. My men are ready to serve you, Avenger. I am a wealthy man who knows the vagaries of this city. It is well known that the treasury's coffers are empty; I can fill them for you. I am wise in the ways of the world and so it is my pleasure to offer myself as adviser. You will find that the problems which beset your rule will be many – more than you can even imagine. I have lived through the hard times of the tyrant's rule and know how to turn things to profit. Money, influence, good counsel, friends in other cities, all these things I offer. Will you take them?' He smiles, his eyes almost lost in the folds of his cheeks. He is undoubtedly a wily fellow who seems to have made a second fortune while the Usurper was sucking the city dry. Will you invite him to step into Star Chamber (turn to **351**), or disappoint him (turn to **288**)?

382

You climb down until you are only a few yards above the beast. You leap down behind it, noiselessly. You are readying to attack it when it sniffs the air again and spins around with a roar, shouting as it spots you, 'Man-thing! I've not eaten manflesh for many a day,' in a thunderous voice, more like the growl of a wolf than the common tongue. However, you have time to hurl a shuriken at it. Its Defence is 6. If you have hit it, roll one die and subtract the result from the monster's Endurance of 19. Turn to **142**.

383

Parsifal clears his throat nervously but when he speaks it is quite clear that he feels there is only one course of action: 'It is surely right to restore the custom of your father and make the shieldmaidens of the Temple to Dama Keepers of the Watch. They enjoy high esteem as keepers of law and order as does my illustrious compatriot, Force-Lady Gwyneth.' Turn back to **373**.

384

The spear-head slashes into its sensitive palate and it pulls up short in pain, giving you time to dive aside. There is a bellow of rage and you see Paladin charging at the dragon, wielding his shining white sword. The dragon whips round to face him, but Paladin delivers a mighty blow and his sword slices through the dragon's scales like a hot knife through butter; black ichor bubbles forth. The dragon rears back in pain, roaring, and Paladin thrusts his sword into its belly. The dragon tries to escape at this point, but Paladin's attack is relentless. With three sword-cuts he shreds one of its wings and soon it is all over. Never have you heard tell of a dragon so easily bested by one man before. At the sight of this the rest of the dragon host breaks off the attack and departs, leaving many dead dragons and men behind. Turn to **360**.

385

The third session of Star Chamber has been called to discuss a pressing matter – the setting of taxes. The currency of governments is the talent, being the weight of a man in pure gold. If Golspiel has been banished, your treasury is full with the weight of twenty-five men in gold. If Golspiel persuaded you not to have him tried by donating ten talents to the treasury, then you have the weight of ten men in gold stored there. In any other case, the treasury is empty. You must now add up the costs facing the Crown:

- Cost of maintaining the Usurper's army if not disbanded – three talents.

- Cost of maintaining the shieldmaidens of Dama, if in the army – two talents.
- Cost of maintaining the shieldmaidens of Dama as City Watch (unless exempted from temple tax) – one talent.
- Cost of maintaining mercenaries as City Watch (paid by Golspiel) – no cost.
- Cost of maintaining the Temple to Nemesis and the Usurper's Watch (paid by the temple) – no cost.
- Cost of maintaining the Order of the Yellow Lotus (regardless of status as City Watch) – one talent.
- Cost of paying Palace servants and messengers – one talent.
- Cost of living in state in the Palace itself – one talent.
- Cost of returning property confiscated by the Usurper to rightful owners – one talent.

When you have calculated how much gold you need and are ready for advice as to how to set taxes, turn to **395**. If the treasury holds enough treasure to meet these costs turn to **415**.

386

Silent as a shade, you drop lithely behind her, a needle already on your tongue. You spit hard and it buries itself right on target. She gasps and stiffens, twisting in pain. Seconds later she is dead, and the two eunuch bodyguards spin around in shocked amazement. You have the initiative, as they stand, scimitars in hand. Will you attack with a Leaping Tiger kick (turn to **66**), an Iron Fist punch (turn to **50**) or a Dragon's Tail throw (turn to **114**)?

387

You decide to follow the advice of the Lord High Steward and retain the services of Foxglove and the Order of the Yellow Lotus. This causes a storm of protest but rumours of a raiding party approaching from the Rift overshadow the importance of your decision to keep the secret informers. You must, however, subtract 2 from your Popularity Rating.

If that now stands at zero or below turn to **315**. If it is above zero turn to **59**.

388

Using your lockpicks you are able to open the lock after a short time. There is a click and the door slides open to reveal a dimly lit corridor stretching away into darkness. Cautiously you step in. The floor and ceiling are polished wood – clean and simple. The walls are of sculpted stone. Carven gargoyles and demonic forms surge out, as if to bite and snap at those that walk this corridor.

Without a sound you glide on down the straight devil-lined corridor, senses alert, your heart beating rapidly. You are stealing into a veritable pit of scorpions. Death lurks ready to pounce upon you, like a wolf-spider on its prey. In the dim light, it seems the sculpted faces and figures mock you silently; as you pass them your spine tingles in anticipation – you half expect them to roar into life and devour you.

After a time, the corridor bends to the right. As quiet as the void, you pause, feet apart and crouch. Carefully you look out and down the corridor. About twelve feet away a figure stands, another ninja guard, beside a door. His back is to you. A sword is strapped to his back. He stands in an attitude of relaxation, yet is unmoving. Will you creep forward and garrotte the sentry (turn to **412**) or hurl a shuriken at his head from the corner (turn to **8**)?

389

As you walk towards Parsifal your suspicions are aroused. Something is not quite right; he looks different in a way you can't quite place. His behaviour in the temple seemed normal enough but there is a tension, well disguised, welling up within him. This may be an imposter. Will you kneel before him as usual (turn to **319**) or knock him to the matting using a Leaping Tiger kick (turn to **329**)?

390

The bolts of energy lance into your side, burning your flesh and causing you to cry out in pain. Lose 6 Endurance. If you still live, you pick yourself up off the floor and approach the Devil-Beast which cowers before you. You are filled with revulsion. A single Tiger's Paw chop finishes the creature off and it slumps to the ground, dead. Immediately, the mist dissipates and, as the sun's rays play upon the beast's body, it begins to shrivel up, until nothing is left but ashes. Resting atop the ashes is a Sceptre of gold, inlaid with many gems. Embossed on its head is a finely carved golden hippogriff. Beside the Sceptre lies a glowing green gem, the Orb. It is not as large as you expected, perhaps the size of an eye. At last, you have found that which you have sought. A great weariness comes over you, for you have battled long and mightily to find these things. You reach down and pick them up. Suddenly everything around you goes white and misty. Turn to **420**.

391

A look of quite childish delight spreads across his unusual face, making him look vulnerable and younger than you had imagined him to be. 'I humbly thank Your Overlordship,' he says. 'This is indeed the highest honour.' He backs away from the throne, bowing three times very low, and knocking into the door-warden who is opening the door to Star Chamber. Note that the Demagogue is now a Privy Councillor on your Charter of Rulership. If you have already appointed four Councillors, turn to **13**. Otherwise you await the next supplicant. Turn to **23**.

Momentarily blinded as you are, you cannot jump aside fast enough, and the sword flashes past, gashing your upper arm. Lose 3 Endurance. If you still live, your vision clears. A short wooden stick drops from the master ninja's sleeve into his hand and he darts forward, raising it to strike without a sound. Will you try to block it (turn to **404**) or allow him to hit you and drive a Leaping Tiger kick into his face while his guard is down (turn to **416**)?

Golspiel's voice is at its most urgent as he says, 'I feel that what this city needs is a group of individuals who have no vested interest in one or other of the temples, a group which can be truly impartial. I shall willingly fund such a group myself. They could, for example, be drawn from the mercenaries in my pay, under their capable and disciplined general, Antocidas.' It is true that you have no money to pay for the Watch until you have raised some taxes, so this may be an important consideration. Turn back to **373**.

Just as you are about to ascend the rock-face that leads up to the base of the crags, a slight sound causes you to turn around. If you have the skill of Arrow Cutting, turn to **28**. If not, turn to **40**.

The issue of taxation is one which touches everybody and you are assailed with requests for audience by all and sundry. The templars to Dama and Avatar demand that the Temple to Nemesis give money back to them, since the Usurper leeched them of their temple funds, while the dark pinnacles of the Temple to the Lord of the Cleansing Flame were gilded with gold leaf. Others clamour for the return of their houses and possessions which were wrongfully seized by the Usurper. Your Privy Councillors are ready to suggest systems which will produce the necessary gold. If you made a deal with Golspiel of the Silver Tongue in return for his support and he gave you a piece of Red Coral in Book 3: *USURPER!*, turn to **405**. If not, turn to **7**.

396

You run at the dragon. Its side is encased in scales. You try to drive the spear between two scales, but you are not skilled with this weapon. The dragon's Defence is 7 and none of your Modifiers apply. If you succeed, turn to **222**. If you fail, turn to **126**.

397

You declare that, for the time being at least, the Order of the Yellow Lotus will continue to serve you and you call your bodyguards to the door. Flanked by them and followed by Foxglove you return to your study, where you ask her what news she has for you. To begin with you can scarcely comprehend her words:

'High Grandmaster Parsifal is dead, Majesty.'

'But I saw him yesterday at evensong – he was in good health for a man of his years.'

'The man you saw leading evensong in the Temple to Kwon the Redeemer was not Parsifal but an imposter.'

'Then who was it?' you demand.

'I have reason to believe that it was none other than Mandrake, Guildmaster of Assassins from the northern city of Wargrave Abbas. A man who reveres Torremalku the Slayer, swift-sure bringer of death to beggar and...' she hesitates, '... king!'

'Where is he now?' you ask.

'Are you not expected for private confessional at the Temple to Kwon this very evening?'

You nod, wondering how she came to know this secret.

'He awaits you. Half a king's ransom, Avenger – I mean Overlord – hangs above your head. Shall I have him dealt with?'

But you reply that you will take the pleasure of killing him yourself (turn to **139**).

398

Silent as a shade, you drop lithely behind her. You chop down and she throws her head back and cries out, before slumping to the ground, out like a light. The two eunuch bodyguards spin around in shocked amazement. You have the initiative, as they stand, scimitars in hand.

Will you attack with a Leaping Tiger kick (turn to **66**), an Iron Fist punch (turn to **50**) or a Dragon's Tail throw (turn to **114**)?

399

Even though you have been relying more upon your wits than your body of late, your reactions have evidently not suffered. You know neither where nor how the Order of the Yellow Lotus obtained the information, but it had warned you truthfully about Mandrake.

His disguise was perfect. Mandrake had killed Parsifal two days before, having already spent some days watching him in secret. He got to know the routine of the temple, and even those closest to the High Grandmaster had been unable to spot him for an imposter. He had even met and talked with Force-Lady Gwyneth about the Order of the Yellow Lotus without arousing her suspicions. He was a formidable foe but you have triumphed again, the first ever to survive the attentions of the Guildmaster of Assassins. You order the monks to select a new High Grandmaster and lead the prayer of thanksgiving for the life and works of Parsifal yourself.

Without Foxglove's help you might well be dead and you send her a message of thanks. Tomorrow there will be a banquet to celebrate your survival.

Turn to **162**.

400

Try as you might, you cannot open the door. You are contemplating using Inner Force to smash it open when a sound behind you causes you to turn. A black-garbed ninja drops into the tunnel. Then the door opens suddenly and another drives a sword at you. You fight for what seems an age, despatching several of the ninja of the Way of the Scorpion, but as soon as you kill one another takes his place. Eventually, you are overwhelmed and Death takes you. You have failed.

401

The Demagogue looks utterly crestfallen when you ask him to leave by the door which leads into the gardens. He pauses indecisively, then stalks out but the look of zeal in his eyes is undimmed. You will do well to keep an eye on his doings, you muse. Turn to **23**.

402

As the battle rages on you hurry down to the harbour-side – nobody is about. You find a suitable boat easily. It has a single sail and looks sturdy and reliable. Soon the city recedes from sight as you head out to open sea. Turn to **79**.

403

Force-Lady Gwyneth stands and bows, then runs a hand through her short spiky, steel-grey hair, before saying, 'In the time of your father, the Loremaster, I served in the Watch that was kept by the shieldmaidens of Dama. It was a happy time for all; crime was driven from the streets. Restore the custom of your father, Avenger – there is no-one in the city who can secure order for you, save I and my shieldmaidens.' She sits and looks down at the table, visibly tense. Turn back to **373**.

404

As the stick comes down there is a click and a sickle-like blade flicks out from its end, but you take the haft on your forearm and jump back. Another deception. You eye each other warily. For the first time you notice a flicker of respect in the Grandmaster's eyes, but he does not speak. Will you close in and attack with a Forked Lightning kick (turn to **30**), a Cobra Strike punch (turn to **18**) or a Teeth of the Tiger throw (turn to **6**)?

Golspiel manages to inveigle himself into your presence when you are breaking fast on the day of the Council. He is dressed all in grey and carries the black arm-bands of mourning and for once does not seem the oily, ebullient character you have come to know. In answer to your enquiry he tells you that his favourite niece died of a sudden coughing attack yesterday: 'So sad, she was so young...' You sympathise and ask him what you can do for him. He rubs his hands together furtively and begins to talk of your agreement:

'Trade is picking up now that the shadow of the Usurper is gone forever. I can make this a prosperous city, Majesty, er... we agreed that I was to become Guildmaster of Merchants.'

If you make Golspiel Guildmaster then all who wish to do business in the city must buy a licence from him. Will you honour your agreement with the merchant (turn to **17**) or go back on your word (turn to **27**)?

Without hesitating, you dive to the ground and roll towards the boulder. It is just as well you did because a thin sliver of steel, glinting in the sun, whirs through the place where you were a moment ago. You recognise it as a shuriken but not of a kind you are familiar with. As you come to your feet, a clipped shout fills the air and a figure dressed as you leaps down from above, a twenty foot fall, to land nimbly before you. As the ninja, for that is what he is, hits the ground he reaches behind his back and draws the short curved sword that lies there. 'You are not of the Scorpion,' he whispers. 'Prepare to die,' and he somersaults forward, to come up slashing at your legs. Nimbly, you leap above the flashing blade and launch an attack of your own.

Will you try to slide under his guard and execute a Dragon's Tail throw (turn to **52**), try a Winged Horse kick (turn to **64**) or try to close in and drive a Cobra Strike up at his throat (turn to **76**)?

407

Who are the members of the bodyguard who never leave your side except within Star Chamber? Are they Onikaba and the samurai (turn to **417**), the shieldmaidens (turn to **39**), or the monks of Kwon (turn to **49**)?

408

Silent as a shade, you drop lithely behind her and whip your garrotte around her neck. She gurgles horribly, hands clutching at the biting wire as you tighten your grip. But her two bodyguards react instantly, turning and slashing you with their scimitars. You are forced to let go of her and engage the eunuchs. Moments later, the priestess casts a spell and you are suddenly engulfed in a sticky web. There is nothing you can do as her guards hack you to pieces.

409

The journey is long and hard. A raiding party of Dark Elves almost capture you as you slink through the Rift-pass but you elude them. The lands you enter beyond the Rift are wild but fertile. A great forest of elms stretches on, seemingly forever.

After many days in the Deeping Woods you skirt the cities of Segesvar and Pest, covering league after league relentlessly until at last you near your goal. Turn to **10**.

410

He stiffens in astonishment. 'You think that I would have any truck with such a thing! Why do you wish for it? Are you a vile worshipper of that spawn of evil, Nullaq? By Rocheval, it is only the fact that you have saved my son's life that prevents me striking off your head this instant! Begone from our fair city, now!' He is apoplectic with rage. Quickly you hurry away. You have no choice but to go to the harbour-side. It is deserted when you reach it – the townsfolk are busy repairing the city. You find a sturdy, single-sailed boat, and set out to sea. Soon the ravaged city of Haven of Tor recedes behind you. Turn to **79**.

An overwhelming sense of *déjà vu* grips you as Solstice materialises from mid-air before the throne once again. The courtiers react exactly as they did when they saw him for the first time; even the gasps of surprise and the whispered asides are the same. Just as before, he bows slowly and says 'Greetings, Overlord. Time is on your side.' Once again, you are staring into the wells of wisdom that are his eyes. Will you reverse your decision and invite him to become a Councillor (turn to **113**) or stick by your earlier decision, if it really was any earlier, and hope that he does not stop time again (turn to **123**) or, if you have had enough of this rigmarole, will you tell Solstice that your answer to him will always be the same even if you have to utter it a thousand million times (turn to **133**)?

A few silent steps bring you within striking range. As fast as a striking mantis you whip the garrotte around the ninja's head, driving your knee into his back, and pull. To your horror, the wire slices straight through the neck and the head topples off to hit the ground with a meaty slap. You start in surprise as the body shatters as it hits the ground. A wax head and a clay body! A trick! A sound causes you to look up. A trapdoor in the ceiling is open and a ninja drops down, with a sai – an iron spike with two sharpened quillons – in each hand. He slashes with one and you duck beneath it, but he follows up with the other, thrusting it at your chest. You try to react but you are caught completely by surprise and you are only able partially to avoid the spike. It bites into your upper arm, causing you to grimace in pain. Lose 5 Endurance. If you still live, the ninja closes for another attack. Instantly, you drive a straight-fingered Cobra Strike at his throat. The Scorpion Ninja's Defence is 7. If you succeed, turn to **20**. If not, turn to **32**.

The Lord High Steward speaks quietly and slowly so that it is almost as if you are hanging onto his every word: 'When the Watch was kept by the shieldmaidens of Dama it did not deter Yaemon from killing the Overlord and paving the way for the Usurper. No! That route has been travelled before. I am convinced a more sensible idea would be to set up a body of people who are able to act impartially. We of Nemesis did just that under the Usurper's rule and assembled a skilled and experienced force. I personally volunteer to scour the Usurper's Watch of what taint remains from your corrupt predecessor, while the Temple to Nemesis is willing to fund the resultant body, should you see the wisdom of this way.'

Turn back to **373**.

414

As you sail on an island looms ahead. A huge galley, a trireme with a single sail and triple rows of oars, comes past. Men dressed in bronze breastplates with greaves and crested helmets with cheekguards stand on deck, their round shields painted in many colours. 'A pirate ship from the island's fleet,' one of the fishermen mutters. However, the ship ignores your tiny fishing vessel. A bustling port opens up as you pass the rocky headland, the Isle of Thieves.

'Perhaps you would like me to drop you here, sir?' asks the captain.

Will you ask him to take you into the island's harbour (turn to **96**) or tell him to take you on to the Haven of Tor (turn to **194**)?

415

You announce in Star Chamber that you have sufficient money in the treasury to meet the Crown costs *as far as you see fit* and that the Council will now discuss who is to be made Strategos in overall command of the Irsmuncast army. As the discussion continues, you abolish the Usurper's unpopular system of marriage licences and restore other minor laws which your father had used when governing. Add 1 to your Popularity Rating.

It is another tenday before the next meeting of Star Chamber and during this period the mood of the city seems fairly calm. You leave the city for the first time on a day's hunting expedition and watch, wryly amused, as your subjects gallop hither and thither pursuing almost anything that moves. You yourself slay a hare with a single shuriken and a great sycophantic roar of approval greets the poor beast's death. You have behaved as an Overlord should and the hunters are happy but, though your bodyguard insists on keeping close to you at all times, a stray arrow passes dangerously close to your head when you are chasing a stag in the woods above the River of Beasts. You return safely to a small hunt banquet.

If Parsifal, High Grandmaster of the Temple to Kwon, is one of your Privy Councillors, turn to **207**. If he is not, turn to **217**.

416

The stick whistles down and you are about to execute a kick when there is a click and a sickle-like blade flicks out from its end. It is too late to block and it sinks into you and out again as your enemy pulls it back. Red agony burns across your shoulder, causing you to stagger back, before you can kick. Lose 4 Endurance. If you still live, the Grandmaster of Shadows pauses, a mocking smile playing about his lips. Will you close in and attack with a Forked Lightning kick (turn to **30**), a Cobra Strike punch (turn to **18**) or a Teeth of the Tiger throw (turn to **6**)?

417

There is a strange spluttering and fizzing sound underneath the oval table and then the whole chamber fills suddenly with smoke. The other Privy Councillors collapse to the floor but you are off your throne and out through the double doors before the noisome fumes can affect you. You slam the doors shut and the two samurai who form your bodyguard at present move to either side of you. Suddenly, the doors are flung open and Parsifal, clutching a wet handkerchief to his face, staggers out into the Throne Room. Will you order the samurai to arrest him (turn to **219**) or rush to him to see if he needs help or healing (turn to **229**)?

Your keen eyesight picks out a strange inconsistency in the weave of the grass, just discernible in the moonlight. You can make out a square outline as if of a turfed-over pit, just ahead of you and slightly to the right. Will you walk up to it and open it (turn to **232**), turn around and walk backwards past it, so you are facing the pit but still heading towards the stone wall (turn to **244**) or walk past the pit a few feet and crouch down, facing the pit (turn to **256**)?

Mandrake had killed Parsifal two days before, having already spent some days watching him in secret. He got to know the routine of the temple, and even those closest to the High Grandmaster had been unable to spot him for an imposter. He had even met and talked with Force-Lady Gwyneth about the Order of the Yellow Lotus without arousing her suspicions. He was a formidable foe but you have triumphed again, the first ever to survive the attentions of the Guildmaster of Assassins. You order the monks to select a new High Grandmaster and lead the prayer of thanksgiving for the life and works of Parsifal yourself. Turn to **162**.

After a long, cold moment of utter silence the mist clears, but only partly, to reveal stone flags underfoot and a familiar battlement. For a time the shadowy outlines of a building which looks like Quench-heart Keep appear through the gloom. The mist clears a little more and you sigh contentedly; the battlements are those which ornament the roof of your Palace in Irsmuncast nigh Edge. The Sceptre or Orb, or both, have transported you back magically from the Elemental Sea. On realising where you are you begin to survey the city. The mist is, in fact, smoke drifting across from the Edgeside. Irsmuncast is burning. You peer down on Palace Road; the lime trees have been cut down. The street is full of Dark Elves and Orcs. Evil has come. Fear for your people grips you. Has the city been over-run?

As you turn to the staircase which leads to the Throne Room a large black raven flaps slowly towards you, bearing a small silver cylinder in its cruel beak. It perches on the battlement, opens its beak and lets the cylinder fall to the stone flags before you. You pick it up as the raven caws twice, loudly and derisively, before flapping away through the mist-like smoke. Inside the hollow silver tube is a message:

'Avenger – an old score shall be settled. The Legion of the Sword of Doom shall conquer the City of Irsmuncast and bring its people into slavery. I swear by Sorcerak to kill you with my own hands – Honoric.'

This is dire news indeed but will you even have the remnants of an army to lead against the Black Legion? A great wail goes up from somewhere in the streets below...

Continued in the Way of the Tiger 5: *WARBRINGER!*

If you enjoyed *Overlord!* then you may like to try these other classic adventure gamebooks from Fabled Lands Publishing.

FABLED LANDS

A sweeping fantasy role-playing campaign in gamebook form

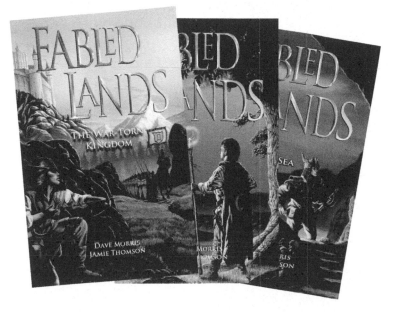

Set out on a journey
of unlimited adventure!

FABLED LANDS is an epic interactive gamebook series with the scope of a massively multiplayer game world. You can choose to be an explorer, merchant, priest, scholar or soldier of fortune. You can buy a ship or a townhouse, join a temple, undertake desperate adventures in the wilderness or embroil yourself in court intrigues and the sudden violence of city backstreets. You can undertake missions that will earn you allies and enemies, or you can remain a free agent. With thousands of numbered sections to explore, the choices are all yours.

The return of BLOOD SWORD —
the groundbreaking multiplayer
gamebook series created by Dave Morris
and Oliver Johnson.

*Every thirteen lunar months the Magi of
Krarth hold a desperate contest to see
which of them will rule that bleak and icy
land. Teams of daring adventurers are
sent down into the labyrinths that lie
beneath the tundra, each searching for
the Emblem of Victory that will win
power for their patron.*

*Only one team can prevail. The others
must die.*

Blood Sword can be played either solo or
in a team of up to four people, combining
the best of role-playing, gamebooks,
novels and boardgames.

Made in the USA
Las Vegas, NV
13 January 2021